The Five-Minute Interview

A Job Hunter's Guide to a Successful Interview

Third Edition

Richard H. Beatty

JOHN WILEY & SONS, INC.

Published by John Wiley & Sons, Inc., Hoboken, New Jersey.
Published simultaneously in Canada.

For general information on our other products and services please contact our Customer
Care Department within the U.S. at (800) 762-2974, outside the United States at
(317) 572-3993 or fax (317) 572-4002.

Wiley also publishes its books in a variety of electronic formats. Some content that appears
in print may not be available in electronic books.

Library of Congress Cataloging-in-Publication Data:

Beatty, Richard H., 1939–
    The five-minute interview: A job hunter's guide to a successful interview / Richard H.
Beatty.—3rd ed.
      p.   cm.
    Published simultaneously in Canada.
    Includes index.
    ISBN 0-471-25083-X (pbk. : alk. paper)
    1. Employment interviewing.   I. Title: 5-minute interview.   II. Title.
HF5549.5.I6B39   2002
650.14—dc21
                                           2002026713

Printed in the United States of America.

10 9 8 7 6 5 4 3 2 1

To my lovely wife, Carolyn, and my fine sons,
Chris and Scott, all of whom I love dearly.

Preface

The world of employment interviewing has undergone dramatic change, rendering the old, traditional techniques of job interviewing ineffective, if not totally obsolete. If you are to successfully compete in this emerging environment, you will need to be keenly aware of these important changes and will also need to be armed with new interview approaches and techniques.

There is a major productivity improvement, organization-effectiveness revolution taking place in American industry today. In response to the ever-intensifying threat of global and domestic competition, and the resultant struggle for economic survival, organizations are striving to achieve quantum improvement in the productivity of their human assets. The continuous wave of corporate downsizing has served to place an added premium on human productivity, as organizations increasingly find themselves in the position of needing to do more, better, and with fewer resources.

Current trends have significantly elevated the importance of employee interviewing and selection as a critical means to achieving organizational goals. There has been a dramatic revival of interest in the development and use of more sophisticated interviewing and selection techniques. This is clearly evidenced in the rush by many companies to embrace the use of core skills and competencies as a means for better measuring and predicting the probable success of employment candidates. In the new, lean, downsized environment, organizations can no longer afford the cost of hiring mistakes. They must get it right the first time.

Further driving employer interest in better hiring techniques are several important studies that document the significant productivity increases that can be realized through improved employee selection. Studies show, for example, that the difference in hiring a "superior" employee over an "average" employee, can often result in productivity gains of 20 percent or higher. One report estimated an average increase in sales volume of +123 percent when hiring "superior" versus "average" sales performers. Such statistics can hardly be ignored!

Organizations are no longer simply content to hire "average" performers capable of "adequate" performance. Instead, they are committed to seeking the "superior" performers—those who have the ability and desire to stretch well beyond traditional job parameters—those who bring about rapid change and quantum improvement in the way the organization carries out its work. These are the leaders and change agents, the ones who the organization is counting on to lead it into the future, and to ensure its survival and success.

This book was written to familiarize you with the nature of current changes, and to equip you with the modern interview strategies required for success in the job market. Its focus is on providing you with specific interview strategies and techniques that will give you a real competitive advantage in this highly competitive, rapidly changing labor market. It is designed for the serious job hunter who is committed to "winning" in the employment interview through the use of effective interview strategies designed to "stack the deck" in your favor.

One such interview strategy is the "five-minute interview." This strategy (described in detail in Chapters 7, 8, and 9) has as its basis a series of key questions to be asked by you during the first five minutes of an interview. These questions enable you to gain important insight into the strategic objectives of the hiring organization and, as a result, structure a highly effective interview approach that can generate real excitement and interest in your employment candidacy.

In Chapter 11 you learn how to discover what the employer considers to be the "ideal" candidate for the position, providing you with significant competitive advantage.

Chapter 12 then outlines a strategy for zeroing in on key problems and challenges the employer feels are most critical to job performance success. This added insight further enhances your competitive advantage in the employment interview by focusing the employer's attention on your ability to add real value in those areas considered to be of major importance to success of the function.

In Chapter 13 you learn how to avoid sure interview disaster, by employing some simple "damage control" principles when sharing "negative" information about yourself in the interview. This chapter also contains helpful tips for avoiding the major interview traps that so frequently result in job interview failure.

This Third Edition includes three new, important chapters:

- Chapter 15 discusses the rapidly growing trend toward competency-based interviewing. It explains how employers go about formulating job competency models for use in assessing candidates during the employment interview. Here you learn the job modeling process that will help you zero in on those competencies employers are likely to use in evaluating you for the position you are seeking.

- Then, in Chapter 16, you learn how to use the same job competency model as the basis for predicting and preparing for a successful behavior-based interview. You learn how to forecast and successfully prepare for both the "technical" as well as "behavioral" questions that are often the principle components of a well-designed, behavior-based interview process. This chapter also provides specific exercises and helpful tips on how to survive and win the behavioral interview game.

- Finally, a new chapter (Chapter 19) on resume preparation has been added. Having a strong resume is critical to interviewing success, and this chapter provides detailed instructions (including specific examples) that clearly illustrate how to prepare a winning resume that will significantly enhance your chances of interview success.

In addition to helping you employ specific techniques for gaining a competitive interview advantage, this book also does a comprehensive job of helping you become familiar (and comfortable) with the interview process in general. Not only will it acquaint you with common interview types and approaches, but its step-by-step, "how to" approach will also prepare you well for the overall employment interview experience. Practical assessment exercises, coupled with some 427 commonly asked interview questions, help build your self-confidence and sharpen your overall interview effectiveness.

I firmly believe that you will find this book to be one of the most comprehensive and informative books on interviewing available on the market today. Whether you are a novice or a veteran interviewee, this book will prepare you well for a highly successful interview experience.

RICHARD H. BEATTY

West Chester, Pennsylvania

Contents

THE
FIVE-MINUTE
INTERVIEW

1

Introduction

Chances are, if you have picked up this book, you will be going on an interview shortly and are interested in learning something that will better prepare you for this important event. This book is intended to do just that!

At this point in time, there are probably a thousand questions going through your mind. What will the interview be like? What type of questions will be asked? What kind of answers are expected? What questions do I need to ask? How do I best sell myself during the interview? What should my approach or strategy be?

This book is designed to answer all of these questions, to help you feel comfortable with the interview process, and to be confident in your skills as an interviewee.

Whether you are a first-time interviewee or a seasoned veteran, you should find this book extremely helpful in sharpening your interviewing skills and effectiveness. Importantly, it will not only provide you with a thorough review of interview basics, but this book will also help you formulate some very effective interview strategies as well. These are geared to the needs of the employer and, if well planned and executed, should serve to generate considerable interest in your employment candidacy. One such strategy is the "five-minute interview," an extremely powerful strategy which is used during the first five minutes of the interview discussion.

One of the major concerns of the interviewee is simply not knowing what to expect in the interview process. Chapters 2, "Types of Interviews," 3, "Interview Techniques," and 5, "Common Interview Questions" are intended to ease this particular concern. These include, for example, a description of the various types of interviews you may encounter, various interviewing techniques frequently used by employers, and a comprehensive list of 427 common interview questions.

To help you prepare for the basic or traditional interview there are two chapters. Chapter 4, "Personal Inventory," will help you to systematically gather the necessary information you will need at your fingertips during the interview. And, finally, Chapter 6, "Basic Interview Strategy," will help you to formulate an effective interview plan that will serve you well in most common interviews.

Since there are currently some very dramatic changes taking place in the world of interviewing, I felt it important to make you aware of these changes and to prepare you to respond effectively to some of the new challenges presented by them.

There is a major cultural revolution now underway in American organizations, as they look for ways to stave off competition and restore competitive health and market preeminence. This has major ramifications for the employment interview process, requiring job candidates to take a much different direction in their interview strategies if they are to compete successfully in the new, emerging environment. Chapters 6 through 9 thoroughly explain these dramatic changes and offer some highly effective interview strategies to counter them successfully.

Chapters 11 and 12 provide additional techniques for helping you to gain a competitive interview advantage. Chapter 11 shows you how to ascertain what the employer considers to be the "ideal" qualifications for the job, while Chapter 12 focuses on the key problems and challenges the employer considers most important to successful job performance. Knowledge in these two important areas is sure to help you put together a "winning" interview strategy.

You are bound to find Chapter 13, "Avoiding Interview Disaster," particularly helpful in avoiding the major pitfalls most frequently associated with interview failure. This chapter provides helpful tips and techniques for effectively dealing with potentially "negative" information about yourself in the employment interview. The inability of a candidate to effectively describe weaknesses, development needs, performance improvement needs, and the like, is perhaps the single most significant cause of interview failure. This chapter will help you confidently share such information with a prospective employer in a way that will prove least damaging to overall interview results.

I believe that you will find Chapter 14 ("Organizational Compatibility") particularly unique. Here you are provided with a very practical approach to follow in measuring how well you are likely to fit into the new work environment—an important aspect of your employment decision.

Chapters 15 an 16 introduce you to the latest trend in interviewing approaches (i.e., the behavior-base interview), and provide helpful advice and tips on how to best prepare for this type of interview. This is a rapidly growing trend, and job seekers need to be fully prepared to answer behavioral interview questions well if they are to successfully compete in today's competitive atmosphere.

Chapters 17 and 18 will provide you with more practical information. This includes a list of questions for you to ask prospective employers as well as a number of practical tips for interviewing.

Finally, Chapter 19 deals with resume preparation and illustrates just how important the resume document is to interview success. Complete instructions for preparing an effective resume have been included and, if followed, should greatly enhance your overall interview effectiveness.

2

Types of Interview

Many interviewees, both inexperienced and seasoned, don't realize that there are several different types of employment interviews. This can be especially disconcerting, and even somewhat unnerving, if you go into an interview expecting the interviewer to utilize a conventional interview approach and find yourself confronted with a totally unfamiliar format. The resulting confusion and associated anxiety that you experience in this unfamiliar setting can sometimes prove devastating to your interviewing effectiveness. What starts out as a good interview experience can suddenly turn into a complete disaster!

A common obstacle to effective interviewing, faced by almost all interviewees, is fear of the unknown. Not knowing what to expect next can suddenly turn an otherwise well-qualified and confident candidate into a "bundle of nerves." As the saying goes, "An ounce of prevention is worth a pound of cure." Knowing what to expect in advance can go a long way toward helping you maintain your self-confidence and composure throughout an interview, regardless of the employer's chosen format.

So that you don't find yourself caught in this kind of predicament, this chapter is intended to acquaint you with the wide range of interview types and formats currently used by employers. Some of these will be readily recognizable, while others, I am sure, will prove totally unfamiliar to you.

It is important to know that, with the increased emphasis on employee productivity and the related need for improved selection techniques, many employers are beginning to experiment more and more with new approaches to the employment interview and selection process. This shift has been accelerated by the fact that there are now a number of new and emerging interview strategies available to the employer, and a number of such strategies is growing yearly.

This chapter is designed to familiarize you with a wide range of interview types or formats. By being able to recognize these, you should have a better sense of where the employer may be headed and thus feel more comfortable with the overall interview process.

SCREENING INTERVIEW

The screening interview, an interview of relatively short duration, is used by the employer to determine whether the employment candidate has sufficient basic qualifications to warrant a more in-depth, formal interview. Normally, the screening interview is conducted by no more than one interviewer and is less than a half hour in duration.

Frequently, the screening interview is conducted by phone as a preliminary step to deciding whether to invite the candidate to the employer's office for a full-blown, in-depth, face-to-face interview. The purpose of this type of interview is to "screen out" unqualified or poorly qualified candidates and thus spare the company the time and expense of an on-site interview.

ONE-ON-ONE INTERVIEW

As the name suggests, the one-on-one interview involves the interviewee and only one representative of the hiring organization, usually the hiring manager (or sometimes the hiring manager's designee). This interview format is normally used by employers when hiring hourly workers or salaried nonexempt employees (secretaries, clerks, etc.) rather than when hiring professional level or managerial employees.

Generally speaking, the one-on-one interview is normally used in those cases when the employer feels that the qualifications and skills of the employee to be hired are clearly defined and fairly easily measured. Therefore, it is seldom used to interview professional or managerial candidates where the selection criteria are far more complex and much more difficult to measure. In such cases the employer is likely to use the group interview approach.

GROUP INTERVIEW

The group interview is by far the most widely used interview approach used by employers when interviewing professional and managerial personnel. In contrast with the one-on-one interview, the group interview involves several representatives of the hiring organization.

In some cases all members of the interview team will meet with the interviewee simultaneously. Much more common, however, team members will meet with the candidate individually and then compare observations about the candidate at a meeting following the interview.

Typically, members of the interview team will include a representative of the personnel department, the actual hiring manager, members of the immediate work group who report to the hiring manager, and, sometimes, the hiring manager's

8

immediate supervisor. When the position in question includes functions that provide services to other "client departments" within the organization, the interview team may also include representatives from this client function as well. Typically, the interview team is comprised of between three to five interviewers but, in the case of key positions or positions where qualifications are unusually difficult to measure, the number of team members may be six or eight.

The group interview subscribes to the theory that "two heads are better than one." It is generally felt by proponents of this approach that by having several persons participate in the interview process, substantially more information can be collected about the candidate than with the one-on-one interview format, thus resulting in a more informed employment decision.

UNSTRUCTURED INTERVIEW

The unstructured interview is a form of group interview where none of the members of the interview team are given a specific assignment or area of the candidate's background to probe. Instead, team members are allowed to freelance and probe whatever areas of the candidate's background they may wish. This is probably the most widely used of the group interview approaches.

Normally, the interview team is provided with a copy of the "candidate specification," a document that sets forth the candidate qualifications sought by the employer. This then becomes the focal point for interview discussions.

An obvious shortcoming of the unstructured interview approach is that the team members may all elect to discuss the same areas, thus leaving important areas of the candidate's qualifications totally unexplored. There is the potential danger that the interview discussions could be concluded without the team members having obtained a balanced overview of the candidate's capabilities. Additionally, the individual interview discussions can get somewhat repetitious, with the same questions being asked of the candidate time and again.

As an interviewee, you need to be alert to these shortcomings, politely advising the team members of their repetition and redirecting discussions toward other important aspects of your overall qualifications.

STRUCTURED INTERVIEW

The structured interview is the exact opposite of the unstructured interview. It is a form of the group interview where each member of the interview team has been given a specific assignment or role. Usually each team member is assigned a specific area of the candidate's background or qualifications to probe in-depth.

Thus, one team member may probe education, another, work experience; another, management style; another, technical depth and so on. Interview assignments are usually made on the basis of those team members who are most experienced or knowledgeable in the specific qualification areas to be probed.

The structured approach to interviewing is generally thought to be a much more thorough and comprehensive approach than the unstructured format. It assures hiring organizations that all important areas of the candidate's qualifications will be thoroughly explored. In addition, there is almost sure to be substantially more overall information collected by the interview team on which to base the final hiring decision. It is believed that this will result in a more informed and dependable employment decision.

The shortcoming of the structured approach is that not all of the members of the interview team are equally skilled in the art of interviewing. Interviewers who are less skilled, therefore, may not investigate critical areas of qualifications as deeply as needed to make a well-founded decision. Here again, as with the unstructured interview, you may need to suggest further discussion in areas you know to be important to the final employment decision.

TARGETED INTERVIEW

The targeted interview is somewhat similar to the structured interview. The difference between the two, however, is that in the targeted interview, the employer identifies key qualifications that are thought to be critical to successful job performance. A conscious decision is made to target these areas for in-depth probing during the interview discussions.

In most cases, interview questions are designed in advance, and team members are accountable for exploring these targeted areas. In this way, nothing is left to chance, and the organization is well-prepared to decide whether the candidate has the necessary qualifications to perform well in these critical selection areas.

The drawback of the targeted interview is that the interview team may tend to be rather narrowly focused and may, therefore, overlook other interesting or exciting qualifications that the candidate possesses which are outside of the areas targeted for in-depth interview focus. Candidates need to be alert to this possibility and may need to carefully guide discussions toward these other areas if the opportunity presents itself.

Situational Interview

The situational interview falls somewhere between being an interview "style" and an interview "technique."

When using the situational approach, the employer selects certain performance dimensions of the position for measurement. For each of these performance dimensions, a situation is defined, either real or hypothetical, which simulates common problems the candidate is likely to encounter on the job.

The candidate is then asked how he or she would handle each of these situations, and the members of the interview team then rate the quality of the candidate's answer against predetermined standards. Additionally, team members make observations about important aspects of the candidate's behavior while addressing each situation presented. These observations include creativity, resourcefulness, conceptual ability, logic, verbal communications skills, and so forth.

The situational interview is becoming an increasingly popular approach. However, although being used with greater frequency, it is rarely used as the only interview approach. More typically, it is being used as one evaluative tool in conjunction with other more conventional interview approaches.

Should you encounter the situational interview, as the interviewee, it is important to remember that the employer is most likely attempting to measure more than the quality of your immediate answer. This is a great opportunity for you to demonstrate your resourcefulness and creativity.

12

ASSESSMENT CENTERS

The use of assessment centers as an interview tool is fairly uncommon, but in some cases they are used by the hiring organization to measure and predict the probability for successful performance of key job elements.

In this type of interview, the employer asks the candidate to actually perform certain key elements of the job in question and then observes how well the candidate can perform them.

A good field for demonstrating how the assessment center approach operates is insurance sales. In such a case the candidate, an applicant for the position of insurance sales representative, is given a homeowner's insurance policy to sell to a potential customer (played by an employee of the company). The candidate is then provided with a list of key features of the policy along with general information about features of competitive policies, and after allowing for some study time is asked to actually sell the policy to the imaginary customer.

Members of the interview team then observe the applicant's presentation, looking for predetermined behavioral and performance standards thought to be critical to successful sales performance. Following this simulation, the interview team members discuss their observations and attempt to predict the probability for successful performance in a real life situation. Unlike the situational interview, the assessment center tries to physically recreate the work environment as well, thus coming as close to a real life situation as possible.

On the surface, this would appear to be an excellent interview approach. However, it should be fairly obvious that few jobs can be so easily simulated. Thus the assessment center approach is not widely used as an interview format, and it is highly unlikely that you will encounter it.

Psychological Assessment

Although not in itself an interview format, psychological assessment is an additional evaluative tool used by some employers to measure the desirability of a particular candidate for a job opening. Some large organizations can afford to have a full-time psychologist on their staff, but most use the services of an outside professional who has been specifically retained for this purpose.

The psychologist will normally require the employment candidate to undergo a battery of tests designed to measure certain skills and aptitudes and will then follow this testing with an in-depth interview. This process can conceivably take the better part of a day to complete. A written report is then provided to the employer which contains an outline of the psychologist's findings, along with appropriate recommendations.

With the exception of relatively high level management positions (i.e., chairman, president, vice president), the use of psychological assessment as an interviewing tool is uncommon. Even at these levels, it is still fairly uncommon.

Stress Interview

Fortunately, the use of the stress interview is also a fairly uncommon practice.

In this type of interview, the employment candidate is intentionally subjected to a great deal of stress so that the members of the interview team can observe how well the candidate can perform under such adverse conditions. The rationale for

14

this approach is the belief that the work environment is a stressful one, and that it is therefore important that the candidate be capable of performing well while under stress.

Typically, the stress interview is conducted in the form of a group interview. The interviewee is normally positioned such that he or she is apart from the interviewers. Usually this means across the table. Interviewers quickly fire a barrage of difficult questions at the candidate, allowing little, if any, time in between for the candidate to gain composure. In this sense, the interview resembles a police interrogation of a criminal suspect. In some cases interviewers may intentionally create conflict by taking issue with something the interviewee has said and aggressively challenging the candidate on this point.

Since very few environments are characterized by a high level of stress on a continuous basis, the stress interview is, in my judgment, of questionable value as an interview strategy. In fact, this format may substantially detract from obtaining meaningful interview results.

The use of stress in the interview can create an unnatural environment that causes the interviewee to feel ill at ease. Stress elicits such emotions as anger, hostility, fear, and so on, which can cause the candidate to react in a less than normal way. What the interview team is observing, therefore, is "abnormal" rather than "normal" behavior. Additionally, stress can seriously impede discussion, causing the interviewee to "clam up" at a time when it is important to get the maximum amount of information on which to base a solid employment decision.

Regardless of my feelings about the use of the stress interview, it is important for you to know that it is an interview style that is used from time to time by certain employers. If you are unfortunate enough to experience it, at least you will know what the interview team is up to. Perhaps this knowledge alone will help you to keep a level of reasonable self-composure that you would not otherwise have had.

We have now concluded a somewhat thorough review of the various interview types used by employers, designed to open your eyes to a number of different approaches that employers may use when interviewing you as a candidate for employment within their organizations. Knowing what to expect should prove helpful in allaying some of your concerns and fears about the evaluation and selection process. In the next chapter, we will address the matter of employer interviewing techniques.

3

Interview
Techniques

If you are currently preparing for your next employment interview, and you are feeling as if you're about to go under the surgeon's knife, don't be afraid—this chapter will provide you with a scalpel of your own. Some of the very same tools that the interviewer/surgeon will use to verbally dissect you to expose the various facets of your qualifications can be applied with equal skill by you in finding out more about your prospective employer.

This chapter has a dual purpose in preparing you to become a more proficient interviewee. The first is to remove some of the fear normally associated with not knowing what techniques the employer will be using to extract information from you. The second is to provide you with some interview techniques of your own that you can use to gather a great deal of relevant information about the employer with whom you will be interviewing, and thereby enable you to make a solid employment decision. Thus, this chapter gives you two for the price of one!

OPEN-ENDED QUESTIONS

The first principle of good interviewing practice is to always ask "open-ended" questions. Open-ended questions are those that require more than a simple "yes" or "no" answer. These are the same kinds of questions that journalists have been well-trained to ask instinctively when gathering information to serve as the basis for a news story. Such questions begin with:

- What
- Where
- When
- Who
- Why
- How

To fully appreciate the effectiveness of open-ended as opposed to "closed-ended" questions (those requiring a simple yes/no answer), consider the following examples:

Closed-Ended: Do you like your current job?

Open-Ended: What do you like about your current job?

Closed-Ended: Does your company provide opportunity for advancement?

Open-Ended: What are the opportunities for advancement in your company? How does this work?

The answers to *open-ended questions* will require providing considerably more information than those requiring just a yes or no answer. As an interviewee, therefore, it should also be very apparent that, when confronted with a seasoned, trained interviewer using the open-ended technique, it will be most difficult for you to get away with simple surface answers. Likewise, by using this technique, it will be equally difficult for the interviewer to avoid providing you with meaningful information.

■

PENETRATION TECHNIQUE

When wishing to probe a given area in greater depth, seasoned employment professionals have been trained to ask a series of open-ended questions in succession. This forces the interviewee into increasing levels of detail and provides the employer with considerably more information on which to base an employment decision. The following are examples of this interview technique:

- *Why* did you resign at Booker Corporation?
- *What* factors led to this decision?
- *How* did you handle this resignation?
- *What* exactly did you say to them?
- *What* are the qualifications you are seeking in a candidate for this position?
- *Why* are these important to job success?
- *How* do you intend to determine the extent of a candidate's technical qualifications?

As you can readily see, the penetration technique is a powerful interview tool for getting to a considerable amount of underlying, and very important, information that can be used in formulating an employment decision. It can be equally effective whether used by the employer or by the job applicant. It is an interviewing technique that is well worth learning!

20

PAUSE/SILENCE

The use of silence or a pause is an effective technique frequently employed by experienced interviewers. It has the effect of compelling the interviewee to talk further on the subject.

Example:

Candidate: "I don't know why things happened that way."

Interviewer: (Silence)

Candidate: "I guess that I could have been better prepared."

This strategy can be equally effective when used by the interviewee, as seen in the following example:

Example:

Employer: "We have a very liberal compensation program."

Candidate: (Silence)

Employer: "Increases have averaged between 8 and 10 percent."

Candidate: (Silence)

Employer: "The highest increase was 19 percent."

REPETITION

When using the repetition technique, the employer simply repeats what the candidate has said in the form of a question. The following are examples of this method:

Example:

Candidate: "I didn't get along with her."

Employer: "Didn't get along?"

Candidate: "No, she was always very critical of me."

Employer: "Very critical?"

Candidate: "Yes, I could never seem to please her, no matter how I tried. She never really liked me."

    The following is an example of how the candidate can also use this interview technique to his or her advantage.

Example:

Employer: "You would like our reporting system."

Candidate: "Like it?"

Employer: "Yes, it doesn't require the kind of detail required as yours, and yet it provides some good control mechanisms."

Candidate: "Control mechanisms?"

Employer: "Yes, with this system it gives you the opportunity to control both volume and cost."

Comparison/Contrast

The comparison/contrast technique is used by the employer to get the employment candidate to talk and to provide more information about a given subject. This technique simply asks the candidate to compare or contrast two or more items or events:

- How would you *compare* your position as a stock analyst with your position as a financial analyst at Corry Bank?
- *Contrast* the management style of your current boss with that of your former boss at Carlton Industries.

As with the previous interview techniques described in this chapter, the comparison/contrast technique can be equally effective when used by the interviewee. Consider the following example:

- How would you *compare* your new performance evaluation system with the old system you described?
- How would you *contrast* the working environment of the credit department to the environment in financial planning? How are they different?

HYPOTHETICAL QUESTION

Employers who have had extensive interview training often make effective use of hypothetical questions as an interview technique. When using this technique, they will structure hypothetical situations or problems and ask the employment candidate to describe how they would handle them. This technique is frequently used by employers in the situational interview approach. The following is an example of the use of hypothetical questions in an interview:

- If you were the plant manager of a small unionized manufacturing plant and caught one of the hourly employees stealing company tools, how would you handle the situation? Assume there were no other witnesses.

The hypothetical question can function as an effective interview tool for the candidate as well. Consider this example:

- If I were an employee and wanted to challenge the performance evaluation given to me by my supervisor, what recourse do I have? Assume, for the moment, that you were my supervisor. What would you tell me?

USE OF EXAMPLES

Interviewers will sometimes ask the candidate to cite examples to support a broad general statement made or to provide greater information on how something was accomplished.

Example:

Candidate: I am considered to be one of the more creative persons in our group.

Interviewer: What examples can you provide of this creativity?

Candidate: We used some participatory management techniques to get the workers more involved and to raise their overall productivity.

Interviewer: Can you give some examples of these participatory techniques? What techniques did you use?

Again, this strategy can prove very helpful to the candidate as well. As the following shows:

Example:

Interviewer: We have promoted employees from project engineer to senior project engineer fairly quickly.

Candidate: That's very encouraging! Can you cite a few examples of recent promotions to this level? Who was promoted? How long did it take?

As readily apparent from this chapter, those interview techniques that have proven very effective for hiring organizations over the years can prove equally as effective for prospective employees. Not only can these techniques be used to skillfully extract and develop more information about you and your qualifications for the position in question, they can be used by you to collect the kind of relevant information required by you to formulate your employment decision as well.

Take some time before your interview to design some questions using the techniques described. By doing so you will substantially improve your interviewing ability and you will acquire considerably more information on which to base your ultimate decision.

An added benefit of this preparation is that you will have considerably greater confidence in your interviewing ability, which will translate ultimately into a more effective presentation. Also, you will create a very favorable impression with the employer, suggesting that you are an exceptionally well-organized, thorough person who is well-prepared and who does not simply accept surface answers to important questions.

4

Personal Inventory

If you are feeling apprehensive about the interview process, relax, you have a lot of company. Interviewing is not a skill that comes easily to most. On the contrary, the great majority of people find it a difficult experience at best. I have seen some very bright, talented, highly successful, and otherwise self-confident individuals rendered almost helpless when faced with the challenge of conducting an effective interview.

I have never ceased to be amazed at how few people give serious thought to advance preparation for the interview experience. Interestingly, this is not the case with the employment resume. Here the would-be employment candidate will frequently seek professional advice and sometimes spend several hours making sure that everything is worded "just right."

But what about the employment interview? Doesn't it warrant just as much advance preparation and attention? After all, the resume simply gets you in the door; it's the interview that you must use to sell yourself!

It should be rather evident from the preceding chapter that there is a lot of information that you will need at your fingertips as you go into the interview. You will need dates, specific job titles, lists of job responsibilities, accomplishments, and the like. Without this information being readily available for instant recall, you will feel extremely uncomfortable and will present the image of someone who is disorganized, someone who has given little thought to what is supposedly a very important event.

Such disorganization may quickly serve to focus the employer's attention on whether this is typical of how ill-prepared you will be for other major events that are of real importance in your career. Can you be counted on to be thorough in carrying out your major job responsibilities, for example? This is certainly not the kind of impression that you will wish to leave with someone who may be in a position to significantly affect your next career step.

Yes, proper advance planning can, and does, have a very real impact on the outcome of the interview process. You simply cannot afford to leave this matter to chance, since your next job, and perhaps your very career, may depend directly on it!

But what are the steps to effective interview planning? What do you need to do to be sure that you will have the kind of information available that will be required during the course of the interview? What does the employment interview planning process look like? These are the key questions that will be addressed in this chapter.

ADVANCE PREPARATION

As with most difficult tasks, the need for advance preparation is paramount. Interviewing is no exception. Before you can effectively proceed with an actual interview, you will need to have a number of facts and details at your fingertips. Further, these facts will have to be organized in such a way that you will be able to recall them instantly when you need them. The advance preparation step, then, is essential to an efficient and orderly interview. It will also save you considerable time and frustration as you proceed with the ensuing conversation.

The following sample forms will help you to organize important interview data in an orderly manner that should facilitate future recall by you during the actual interview process.

EDUCATION

In the spaces provided, fill in all information requested, starting with your most recent degree first:

Degree: _____

School: _____ Date graduated: _____

Major: _____ Grade point average: _____

Honoraries: _____

Scholarships: _____

Extracurricular _____
activities: _____

Offices held: _____

_____

- -

Degree: _____

School: _____ Date graduated: _____

Major: _____ Grade point average: _____

Honoraries: _____

Scholarships: _____

Extracurricular _____
activities: _____

Offices held: _____

_____

- -

PROFESSIONAL RECOGNITION

Provide the information requested in the appropriate spaces:

Patents: Title _____ Number _____ Issue date _____

Title _____ Number _____ Issue date _____

Copyrights: Title _____

Name of publication _____

Publication date _____

Title _____

Name of publication _____

Publication date _____

Professional designation: _____

Date certified: _____

Certifying organization: _____

Professional designation: _____

Date certified: _____

Certifying organization: _____

Honors   Name _____
and
awards: Awarded by _____

Date awarded _____

Name _____

Awarded by _____

Date awarded _____

Name _____

Awarded by _____

Date awarded _____

WORK EXPERIENCE

Starting with your most recent employer first, list all of your previous positions, including dates of employment, title of position held, and key responsibilities. For those instances where you have held more than one position with a given employer, indicate this by writing "same" in the space provided for the employer's name. List all positions held in reverse chronological order (starting with the most recent position first), again providing dates through which the positions were held, and key responsibilities and achievements.

1. Dates employed: From _____ to _____

   Employer: _____

   Division: _____

   Position title: _____

   Key responsibilities: _____

   _____

   _____

   _____

   _____

   Key accomplishments: _____

   _____

   _____

   _____

   _____

2. Dates employed: From _____ to _____
   Employer: _____
   Division: _____
   Position title: _____
   Key responsibilities: _____

   _____

   _____

   _____

   _____

   _____

   Key accomplishments: _____

   _____

   _____

   _____

   _____

   _____

On a separate sheet of paper, continue with this process until you have accounted for all full-time positions that you have held. If a recent college graduate, or an individual with limited work experience, you may wish to include summer employment or other forms of temporary or part-time employment as well.

When describing both your responsibilities and accomplishments, use quantitative terms or descriptions to convey a greater understanding of the magnitude or scope of these important dimensions of your background. Having such quantitative data readily available will add additional credibility to your qualifications and greatly improve the effectiveness of your presentation.

WINNING ATTITUDE

Unquestionably, a winning attitude is critical to successful inter-view performance. If you don't believe that you are a winner, no one else will. Without such confidence, how can you expect to per-suade a veteran interviewer, who sees hundreds of qualified candi-dates, that you are worth hiring? Without positive feelings about yourself and about what you can contribute to a prospective em-ployer, how can you expect to succeed in such a highly competitive environment?

The key to establishing a positive attitude and improved self-confidence is to take the time to be introspective, to look within yourself for a sense of value. What is it that you have that will truly add value to the employer's organization? What is it that you may have to contribute that others may not? Such "added value" can take many forms, including the following:

1. Ability to solve key issues and problems.
2. Ability to bring new ideas, change, and improvement to the organization.
3. Ability to motivate and lead others to achieve high stan-dards of excellence and productivity.
4. Ability to define key opportunities for cost reduction.
5. Ability to spot key opportunity areas for expansion and increased profitability.
6. Ability to design new, innovative, and cost-saving com-puter software systems.

These are but a few of the many ways that an individual may add value to a prospective employer's organization. Obviously, the ac-complishments that you have identified earlier in this chapter offer prime examples of areas through which you might add value to your new organization. But what else do you have to contribute? Hopefully, the following exercises will help you to define key areas of strength and ability that you can use to effectively bolster your sense of self-worth and improve your overall interviewing effectiveness.

DEFINING YOUR VALUE

If you were to ask a group of close associates or friends to describe your greatest attributes, how would they describe you? What adjectives would they use? List them:

_____   _____
_____   _____
_____   _____
_____   _____
_____   _____

Now go back and list these adjectives from 1 to 10, based on how you believe your friends or associates might rank them. Use number 1 to represent the adjective that you feel these persons would choose to best describe you, with number 10 representing the adjective that describes you least.

In your judgment, what things are there about your behavior, skills, and/or achievements that has caused these individuals to describe you in this way? List these:

Positive behavior/skills/achievements: _____

_____

_____

_____

_____

_____

_____

Considering these factors, what appear to be your greatest strengths? Describe these strengths in terms of specific skills, knowledge, and personal attributes.

Strongest skills: _____

_____

_____

_____

_____

Greatest knowledge: _____

_____

_____

_____

_____

Personal strengths: _____

_____

_____

_____

_____

_____

_____

Now, rank these from those of greatest strength to those of least strength.

The preceding exercise should be repeated several times using different groups of people. For example, try using previous bosses, former professors, and even members of your immediate family.

From a business perspective, what are the things that you do with greatest proficiency? List them:

Do best: _____

_____

_____

_____

_____

_____

What is there about you that enables you to perform well in these areas? List the special skills and abilities that you possess that enable you to do so:

_____

_____

_____

_____

_____

_____

In reviewing your life to date, what would you list as being your most significant accomplishments? Of which of your overall achievements are you most proud? List these accomplishments in each of the three categories shown:

Education: 1. _____

2. _____

3. _____

Business: 1. _____
2. _____
3. _____

Personal: 1. _____
2. _____
3. _____

CONCLUSION

Take a few minutes now to reflect on the information that you have provided in each of the preceding exercises. It is highly likely that you have been successful in identifying a number of strengths and accomplishments—things that could be very valuable to a future employer. Having done this, take a few more minutes to answer the following important questions:

1. Why do I deserve the position for which I will be interviewing?
2. Which of my overall strengths, accomplishments, and personal attributes best qualifies me for this position?
3. Considering all of this, what should I be prepared to tell a prospective employer about my overall qualification?

Having concluded the exercises in this chapter, you now have defined your "personal inventory"—those key dimensions of your overall qualifications on which you will be readily able to draw during the course of the actual employment interview. Certainly, you are now better prepared to successfully address many of the basic kinds of interview questions that most employers will likely throw at you.

Chapter 5, "Common Interview Questions," prepares you even better for your interview experience.

5

Common Interview Questions

Of all the things about the job hunting process that strike fear into the heart of the candidate, it is usually the employment interview that is the most paralyzing. What are they going to ask me? What am I going to need to know? Although an individual may be enormously well qualified and generally self-confident about his or her abilities, there is still a tendency to feel a little "naked" when going into the interview process.

There seems to be a fairly high correlation between the amount of time that has lapsed since a person's last interview and the level of anxiety experienced in facing the next one. The longer the time lapse, the higher the anxiety level. If your last interview was 15 or 20 years ago, the feeling may be something close to panic; if you are a newcomer to the employment market, the very thought of your first interview can cause a huge lump to well up in the pit of your stomach and may elevate your anxiety level to one notch below sheer terror! I know. I remember my first employment interview all too well.

Relax, it really needn't be that bad. There are some things that you can do to substantially reduce, if not all but eliminate, the preinterview jitters. This chapter should go a long way toward restoring calm and a reasonable level of self-confidence and control.

Interview anxiety, as with many types of fears, has its principal roots in the unknown. Those who have been away from the interview process for a number of years, and those who are about to experience their first interview, simply don't know what to expect.

To help you to address these concerns, we have already discussed interview types and interview techniques in the preceding chapters. This chapter deals with the one remaining area of concern — "What are the questions that I will be asked?"

Although it would be impossible to list all of the questions that one might conceivably encounter during the course of an employment interview, the list I have compiled in this chapter is one of the most extensive anywhere. You should never expect to experience all of these questions in a single interview; in fact, there are some that you may never encounter.

In this chapter, we list 427 commonly asked interview questions. For ease of reference, they have been divided into 5 major categories:

1. Education.

2. Work experience.

3. Management effectiveness.

4. Personal effectiveness.

5. Miscellaneous.

You might compare having this list to having the final examination questions in advance. If you are able to provide good answers to the majority of these questions, you will be exceptionally well-prepared to handle a very high percentage of the interviews you will encounter — including the very toughest. This should go a long way toward eliminating your jitters and replacing the anxiety with self-confidence.

In order to reap the full benefit from this chapter, go through it first several times on your own. Once you have reached the point where you feel relatively comfortable with your answers, go through them aloud with a close friend. Have your friend provide you with some feedback and assist you in formulating answers that will position your employment candidacy in the best possible light.

As an additional measure, I would strongly recommend that you focus additional time and effort on those questions that you find the most difficult. If it is a critical question, and both you and your friend have difficulty in formulating a satisfactory answer, seek the counsel of a seasoned employment professional.

EDUCATION

Your educational background is often the source of many questions, starting with high school and going up to graduate school. Examples of these questions are:

High School

1. Where did you go to high school?
2. When did you graduate?
3. What kind of student were you?
4. How were your grades?
5. What was your class rank?
6. In what extracurricular activities did you participate?
7. What leadership role did you play in any of these activities?
8. What student offices did you hold, if any?
9. What honors or awards did you receive?
10. What courses did you enjoy most? Why?
11. What courses did you enjoy least? Why?
12. In which courses did you get your best grades? Why?
13. In which courses did you have your worst grades? Why?
14. What did you learn from your high school education?

15. Who most influenced you during your high school years?

16. In what ways?

17. How would you describe yourself during your high school years?

18. What adjectives would you use?

19. How satisfying were your high school years?

20. What aspects were most satisfying? Why?

21. What aspects were least satisfying? Why?

22. What did you do in your spare time?

23. What personal activities or hobbies were you involved in?

24. What full- or part-time jobs did you have?

25. How well did your high school education prepare you for college?

26. For life in general?

College

1. Which university/college did you attend?

2. When did you attend _____ University/College?

3. How did you come to select _____ University/College?

4. What were the factors that influenced your decision?

5. What was your major?

6. When did you decide to major in _____ ?

7. What were the factors that led to this decision?

8. What other majors did you consider?

9. What led you to choose _____ over these?

10. Did anyone influence your decision to attend University/College? If so, who?

11. In what ways did they influence you?

12. If you could go back in time, would you choose a different school? Why?

13. If you could go back in time, would you select a different major? Why?

14. What would it be? Why?

15. Did you have a minor?

16. What was it?

17. Why did you choose this as your minor?

18. What kind of student were you?

19. How were your grades?

20. What was your overall grade point average?

21. What was your grade point average in your major?

22. What was your grade point average in your minor?

23. What accounted for your low (or high) grade point average?

24. In what courses did you do best? Why?

25. In what courses did you do worst? Why?

26. Which courses did you most enjoy? Why?

27. Which courses did you least enjoy? Why?

28. What academic honors or awards did you receive? Describe.

29. What scholarships or grants did you receive? Describe.

30. In what extracurricular activities did you participate?

31. What leadership role (if any) did you play in these activities? Explain.

32. What student offices have you held, if any? When?

33. How were you selected for such offices?

34. Approximately how much time did you study each week?

35. What did you do in your spare time?

36. Did you work full- or part-time while in school?

37. When and where did you work?

38. How did you pay for your college education?

39. For what portion did you pay? How?

40. How has your college education prepared you for your career?

41. How has your college education prepared you for this position?

42. How has your college education prepared you for life, in general?

43. What aspects of your college education did you enjoy most?

44. What aspects of your college education did you least enjoy? Why?

45. Who most influenced you during your college years?

46. In what ways?

47. As a college student, how would you describe yourself? What adjectives would you use?

48. In what ways are you still the same?

49. In what ways are you different? Why?

Graduate Education

1. Which university/college did you attend?

2. When did you attend _____ University/College? Dates?

3. Why did you decide to go to graduate school?

4. What factors led to this decision?

5. How did you come to select _____ University?

6. What were the factors that led to this decision?

7. What were the factors that caused you to select as your major?

8. Were you considering any other majors?

9. What were they?

10. What factors caused you to select _____ rather than these other majors?

11. Has this proven to be a good choice? Why?

12. If you could go back in time, would you change it? If so, to what would you change it? Why?

13. What kind of student were you?

14. How were your grades?

15. What was your grade point average?

16. What academic awards or honors have you received?

17. What scholarships or grants have you received? Describe.

18. In which courses did you get your best grades? Why?

19. In which courses did you get your worst grades? Why?

20. Which courses did you like most? Why?

21. Which courses did you like least? Why?

22. What is the title of your thesis?

23. What factors led to your selection of this topic?

24. What research have you done to support your thesis?

25. What were the results of this research?

26. What are the major findings and conclusions of your thesis?

27. Who was your thesis advisor?

28. What was this person's role?

29. What resources and support did you have available to support your thesis project?

30. What were some of the toughest questions asked during your dissertation?

31. Why were these questions particularly tough?

32. What were your answers to those questions?

33. What additional graduate research have you done?

34. Has your graduate work led to any other publications? What are the titles, the names of publications and publication dates?

35. Do you hold any copyrights? Describe.

36. Has your graduate work led to any patents? Describe. What are the patent titles and issue dates?

37. In what extracurricular activities did you participate?

38. Did you play a leadership role in any of these? Explain.

39. What student offices have you held, if any? When?

40. How were you selected for such offices?

41. Approximately how much time did you study each week?

42. Did you work full- or part-time while you were in graduate school? Discuss.

43. Where and when did you work?

44. What did you do in your spare time?

45. How did you pay for your graduate education?

46. What portion did you pay for? How?

47. How has your graduate education prepared you for your career?

48. In what manner has your graduate education prepared you for this position?

49. What aspects of your graduate education did you most enjoy? Why?

50. What aspects of your graduate education did you least enjoy? Why?

51. If you could go back in time, what is there about your graduate education that you would do differently? How would you change it, and why?

52. Who had the greatest influence on you during your graduate years?

53. In what ways were you influenced?

54. How do you feel your fellow students would have described you while in graduate school? What adjectives would they have used?

WORK EXPERIENCE

Questions regarding your work experience delve into your current position, past positions, and miscellaneous areas regarding your employment experience. Samples of these questions are:

Current Position:

1. What circumstances led to your employment by the _____ Company?
2. What factors influenced your decision to work there?
3. What were the dates of your employment?
4. Are you still employed there?
5. What is your job title?
6. Describe the general organizational structure.
7. Where do you fit in?
8. To whom do you report (name and title)?
9. To whom does your supervisor report (title)?
10. What are the titles of the other positions that report directly to your supervisor?
11. How many employees do you manage?
12. What are the titles of those who report directly to you, if any?
13. What are the titles of those who report indirectly to you, if any?
14. What are your functional responsibilities?
15. What business functions do you manage directly? Explain.

16. What business functions do you manage indirectly? Explain.

17. What are the financial dimensions of your position (i.e., budgets, sales volume, cost of goods manufactured, etc.)?

18. What are your key responsibilities or objectives?

19. Generally, how well have you performed toward these objectives?

20. Toward which of these objectives have you performed particularly well? Why?

21. Toward which of these have you performed least well? Why?

22. In what ways could your performance be improved? Describe.

23. What steps have you taken to improve your performance in these areas?

24. What additional plans do you have for improvement?

25. What have been your major accomplishments while in this position?

26. Why were these important?

27. What impact have they had on the organization?

28. What was your specific role in these accomplishments?

29. Did others contribute to these results?

30. What role did they play?

31. Which aspects of this position do you enjoy most? Why?

32. Which aspects of this position do you enjoy least? Why?

33. Which aspects of the job do you perform best? Why?

34. Which aspects of the job do you perform least well? Why?

35. What are the major problems or challenges currently faced by your group?

36. What plans do you have for addressing these problems?

37. What approaches need to be tried? Why?

38. What results would you anticipate? Why?

39. How do you see your job changing over the next couple of years? Why?

40. What are you currently doing to prepare for these changes?

41. How would you describe your current supervisor? What adjectives would you use to describe him or her?

42. How would you describe your supervisor's management style?

43. How would you describe your relationship with your supervisor?

44. Which aspects of your supervisor's management style/philosophy do you like most? Why?

45. Which aspects of your supervisor's management style/ philosophy do you like least? Why?

46. How do you address these negative aspects?

47. Do you have a formal performance evaluation system? How does it work?

48. What is the basis for evaluation?

49. What are the various rating levels?

50. What was your most recent rating?

51. What reasons were given for this rating?

52. How did you feel about this rating?

53. Was it fair or unfair? Why?

54. In which areas of your performance was your supervisor most complimentary? Why?

55. In which areas of your performance was your supervisor the most critical? Why?

56. Do you agree with this criticism? Why or why not?

57. What have you done to improve your performance in these areas?

58. What have been the results of your efforts?

59. What is your current compensation level?

60. What is the date of your next salary review?

61. Does the _____ Company have a formal salary review program?

62. At what intervals are employee salaries reviewed?

63. What was the date of your last review?

64. What is the typical range of salary increases granted?

65. What was the percentage of your last increase?

66. Was this considered a good increase? Explain.

67. How do you feel about the amount of this increase compared to your level of contribution?

68. What do you feel your next increase will be? Why?

69. Why do you wish to leave the _____ Company? What factors have led to this decision?

Past Positions

The following should be answered for each significant position you have held.

1. What was your job title?

2. How did you acquire this position?

3. What were the circumstances that led to this assignment?

4. Was this move considered to be a promotion, a lateral move, other? Explain.

5. Did you receive a salary increase at the time of this move? How much (dollars and percentage)?

6. Was this considered a good increase? Explain.

7. What were you told were the reasons why the company elected to move you to this assignment?

8. How did you feel about this move?

9. Was it in keeping with your career objectives?

10. What were the dates of your tenure in this position?

11. To whom did you report (name and title)?

12. Describe the organizational structure.

13. How many employees did you manage, if any?

14. What were the titles of those who reported directly to you, if any?

15. What were the titles of those who reported to you indirectly, if any?

16. What were your functional responsibilities?

17. What were the financial parameters of your position (i.e., budgets, sales volume, cost of goods manufactured)?

18. What were your key responsibilities or objectives?

19. Generally, how well did you perform toward these objectives?

20. Toward which of these objectives did you perform particularly well? Why?

21. Toward which of these objectives did you perform least well? Why?

22. What aspects of your overall performance could have been improved? How? In what way?

23. What were your most significant accomplishments?

24. Why were these significant?

25. What positive impact did they have on the organization?

26. What was your specific role in these accomplishments?

27. What aspects of this position did you enjoy most? Why?

28. What aspects of this position did you enjoy least? Why?

29. What were your performance ratings while in this position?

30. How did you feel about these ratings? Why?

31. Of which aspects of your performance was your supervisor most complimentary? Why?

32. Of which aspects of your performance was your supervisor least complimentary? Why?

33. What adjectives would you use to describe your former supervisor?

34. How would you describe your supervisor's management style/philosophy?

35. Generally, how would you describe your relationship with your supervisor?

36. What aspects of your supervisor's style/philosophy did you like most? Why?

37. What aspect of your supervisor's style/philosophy did you like least? Why?

38. What did you do to deal with this?

39. Why did you leave this position?

40. What were the circumstances that led to your next assignment?

41. Why did you leave the _____ Company?

42. Was it a voluntary or involuntary separation?

43. What were the factors that led to this separation?

44. If we talked to your former supervisor at the _____ Company, what do you feel he would say about you and your performance?

Miscellaneous Work Experience

1. Of the employers for whom you have worked, which did you like most? Why?

2. Of the employers for whom you have worked, which did you like least? Why?

3. Of the positions you have held, which did you like most? Why?

4. Of the positions you have held, which have you enjoyed least? Why?

5. Of your past supervisors, whom did you like most? Why?

6. Of your past supervisors, whom did you like least? Why?

7. Of the various environments in which you have worked, in which were you most productive?

8. What was there about this environment that accounted for this high level of productivity?

9. Of the various environments in which you have worked, in which were you least productive?

10. What was there about this environment that accounted for this reduced productivity level?

11. How would you compare these two environments?

12. In what ways were they the same?

13. In what ways were they different?

14. What factors accounted for higher productivity?

15. What factors accounted for lower productivity?

16. What does this tell you about the kind of environment in which you will be most productive?

17. What does this tell you about the kind of environment in which you will be least productive?

18. How would you compare your past positions?

19. Which did you like most? Why?

20. Which did you like least? Why?

21. Which of your past positions has best prepared you for this job? Why?

22. In what ways has it prepared you?

23. What aspects of other positions that you have held have helped prepare you for this job? How?

24. What do you consider to be your greatest technical strengths? Why?

25. In what technical areas do you feel you need more development to become proficient?

26. What development plans do you have to address these areas?

27. In general, how qualified do you feel to perform this position?

28. With which aspects of the position do you feel most comfortable? Why?

29. With which aspects of the position do you feel least comfortable? Why?

30. What specific capabilities do you bring to the job that should prove helpful? Why?

31. What specific capabilities do you lack that are required for successful performance of this position?

32. Do you consider these critical? Why or why not?

33. What do you plan to do about these deficiencies?

34. What would be your overall job strategy or approach?

35. What would be some of the first things that you would do? Why?

36. What things would you save for later? Why?

37. If you were the _____ Company, would you hire you for this position? Why?

38. What would be your greatest concern about your candidacy? Why?

39. On a scale of 1 to 10 (1 = low, 10 = high), how would you rate your probability for successful performance in this position? Why?

MANAGEMENT EFFECTIVENESS

1. How would you describe your management philosophy?

2. What do you believe good management is?

3. What do you believe is characteristic of bad management?

4. How would you describe your management style?

5. What aspects of your management style are consistent with your management philosophy? Why?

6. What aspects of your management style are inconsistent with your management philosophy? Why?

7. What techniques do you use to manage others?

8. What do you believe is the proper balance between employee freedom and management control? Describe.

9. What do you do to encourage employee freedom and participation in organizational decisions?

10. What kinds of decisions do you delegate to others? Why?

11. What kinds of decisions do you reserve for yourself? Why?

12. What criteria do you use to measure subordinate performance?

13. How do you go about monitoring subordinate performance?

14. What managerial controls do you use?

15. How do you exercise these controls?

16. What is your human resources philosophy? What is your belief about the role of people in the organization?

17. How would your subordinates describe your management style? What adjectives would they use?

18. What would they likely cite as your managerial strengths? Why?

19. What would they likely cite as areas in which you could improve as a manager? Why?

20. In what ways would you agree with their evaluation? Why?

21. In what areas would you disagree with their evaluation? Why?

22. What techniques do you employ to motivate subordinates?

23. How do you go about rewarding good performance?

24. What kind of things do you do?

25. How do you go about handling poor subordinate performance?

26. What are your beliefs about training and development? Why?

27. What process do you use for evaluating the training and developmental needs of subordinates?

28. What do you do to meet these needs?

29. What do you believe is the difference between management and leadership?

30. Do you consider yourself a better manager or a better leader? Why?

31. Describe your planning process.

32. What is your planning cycle? Why?

33. Who participates in your planning process? Why?

34. How effective is your planning process?

35. What aspects are particularly good? Why?

36. What aspects could stand improvement? Why?

37. What steps are you taking to improve this process?

38. Do you have functional objectives?

39. How are these objectives established?

40. Who establishes them?

41. How often do you report progress against these objectives?

42. What is the method for reporting such progress?

43. What overall resources do you have at your disposal to carry out your job responsibilities?

44. How effectively do you manage these resources?

45. How do you go about managing these resources effectively?

46. How do you go about monitoring and controlling the use of these resources?

47. Which resources are best managed? Why?

48. Which resources could be better managed? Why?

49. What plans do you have for improving resource management?

50. How would your supervisor describe your management style? What adjectives would he or she likely use? Why?

51. About which areas of your management style would he or she likely be most complimentary? Why?

52. About which areas of your management style would he or she likely be most critical? Why?

53. Would you agree or disagree with these observations? Why?

54. What do you consider to be your greatest strengths as a manager? Why?

55. What do you consider to be your greatest shortcomings as a manager? Why?

56. What are you doing to improve in these areas?

57. Overall, on a scale of 1 to 10 (1 = low, 10 = high), where would you rate your managerial effectiveness? Why?

PERSONAL EFFECTIVENESS

1. How would you describe yourself? What adjectives would you use?

2. What do you consider to be your greatest strengths or attributes? Why?

3. In what areas could you most improve?

4. If we had three or four of your peers who know you well in this room, how would they describe you? What adjectives would they likely use?

5. What would they list as your key strengths? Why?

6. What areas would they suggest for improvement? Why?

7. In past performance evaluations, what have your supervisors had to say about your personal effectiveness?

8. What adjectives or traits have they used to describe your personal style?

9. In what areas have they been particularly complimentary? Why?

10. In what areas have they indicated the need for improvement? Why?

11. In what ways are you trying to improve yourself?

12. How would you categorize your overall personality type—very aggressive, somewhat aggressive, or passive? Why?

13. Would you classify yourself as a hard driving or relatively laid back personality? Why?

14. How does your personality type manifest itself in the work environment?

15. Who is your best friend? Why?

16. What traits do you like and admire about this person?

17. Who is the person you like least? Why?

18. What characteristics or traits do you dislike about this individual? Why?

19. How do you handle interpersonal conflicts?

20. Do you challenge and confront conflict or do you avoid it?

21. How do you go about confronting others?

22. How do you go about avoiding conflict?

23. Of your past supervisors, whom did you like most? Why?

24. What were the traits or characteristics that you liked about this supervisor? Why?

25. Of your past supervisors, whom did you like least? Why?

26. What were the traits or characteristics that you least liked about this individual?

27. In general, how do you feel about yourself?

28. If there was something that you could change about yourself, what would it be? Why?

29. In what ways would you change yourself? To what? Why?

30. With what aspects of your life are you most happy? Why?

31. With what aspects of your life are you least happy? Why?

32. What are you doing to improve these areas?

33. What are your short-term career objectives? Why?

34. In general, how do you feel about your progress toward satisfying these objectives?

35. In what areas have your objectives been met?

36. In what areas have you fallen short of your objectives? Why?

37. What are your long-term career objectives? Why?

38. In general, how do you feel about your progress toward realization of these objectives?

39. In what areas have these long-term objectives been met?

40. In what areas have you fallen short of these objectives? Why?

41. To what extent is this position relevant to your career objectives?

42. In what manner does it support or complement these objectives?

43. In what ways is it not relevant?

44. How do you feel about this?

45. How would you describe your level of interest in this position?

46. How would you characterize the ideal work environment?

47. How well does this profile match with what you perceive to be the environment here at the _____ Company?

48. In what ways does it appear to be a good match?

49. In what ways might it fall short?

50. How do you spend your spare time?

51. What hobbies or activities do you enjoy?

52. Are you active in the community?

53. In which community organizations are you involved, if any? What is the nature of your involvement?

54. Do you hold any community or public offices? If so, in what organizations, and for how long?

55. What self-improvement plans do you have?

56. What are you now doing to improve yourself?

MISCELLANEOUS

The following are miscellaneous questions that an interviewer might ask.

1. How would you describe the perfect job? What would be characteristic of such position?

2. Why are you interested in this position?

3. What aspects of this position most interest you? Why?

4. What aspects of this position least interest you? Why?

5. How long do you feel you would continue to be challenged in this position? Why?

6. How satisfied do you feel you would be in this position? Why?

7. What concerns do you have about this position?

8. In general, how would you describe your level of interest in this position?

9. Why should we hire you for this position?

10. What do you feel you have to offer?

11. Why do you want to work for the _____ Company?

12. What do you feel we have to offer that others do not?

13. How active have you been in the job market?

14. How long have you been looking?

15. If I may ask, what other offers have you received?

16. How would you compare this position with others that you are currently considering?

17. What is your current compensation level?

18. What are your compensation requirements?

19. With what references can you provide me? Describe your relationship with each.

20. How long have you known each of your references?

21. What do you feel your references will have to say about you? Why?

22. For your years of experience, why aren't you in a higher level position?

23. For your years of experience, your compensation level seems on the low side. Why?

24. Does your employer know you are seeking other employment?

25. What discussions have you had with your current employer regarding your job/career concerns and objectives?

26. What have been the results of such discussions?

27. How soon do you need to hear from us? Why?

28. How is your general health?

29. Do you have any major health problems that would impede your ability to perform this job?

30. If so, what is the nature of these limitations?

31. In what manner may these restrictions impede or hinder your ability to perform the job?

32. Are there any remaining questions that you would like to ask?

33. Is there anything else you feel is important for me to know about you?

6

Basic Interview Strategy

Up to this point, we have been dealing with the mechanics of interviewing. We are now going to change our perspective and move on to the topic of interview strategy. In this chapter we will be discussing basic, commonly used interview strategy.

Let's first explore the fundamental interview strategy frequently employed by organizations and candidates alike. Having mastered this basic strategy, we will then move on to the more advanced techniques.

If one is to be successful in planning a winning interview strategy, there must first be some reasonable understanding of the employer's strategy. Only if you possess an understanding of the interviewer's strategy can you realistically expect to plan and carry out a successful counterstrategy designed to win.

Can you imagine the Dallas Cowboys or the Washington Redskins going into the Super Bowl, for instance, without at least some idea about the game strategy likely to be employed by their opponent? This would be pure suicide! Likewise, as an employment candidate, you need to have some reasonable expectation as to what the employer will do in the interview process, if you are serious about developing your own winning counterstrategy. In developing your interview strategy, therefore, you must first start with understanding the employer's interview approach. This is where we will start.

INTERVIEW THEORY

By definition, the employment interview is a two-way discussion between a job applicant and a prospective employer with the objective of exploring the probable compatibility between the applicant's qualifications and the needs of the employer, for the purpose of making an employment decision. It is the intent of both parties during this discussion to gain as much relevant information as possible on which to base this decision. Further, it is their intent to use the information obtained during the interview process to predict, with some level of accuracy, the probability for a successful match.

Modern interview theory subscribes to a single, universal theory around which almost all employment selection processes are designed. This theory is as follows:

> Past performance and behavior are the single most reliable factors known in predicting future performance and behavior.

With this theory in mind, it is important for the interviewee to know that the employer's basic interview strategy will be to use the interview discussion to uncover past performance and behavioral evidence in those areas that the employer considers important to successful job performance. These important areas are commonly known as selection criteria. It is against these criteria that the employer will be comparing the qualifications of prospective candidates, and eventually arriving at a final employment decision.

It should be evident that, as the candidate, it will be necessary for you to get some definition of these selection criteria if you expect to be successful in developing an effective counterstrategy. The key to accomplishing this is to force yourself to think as the employer does. Specifically, the question to ask is, "How does the employer go about developing candidate selection criteria?"

DEVELOPING THE CANDIDATE SPECIFICATION

The first step used by the employer in structuring an interview strategy is usually development of what is commonly known in professional employment circles as the candidate specification. This document typically describes the candidate sought by the employer in terms of such qualifications as knowledge, skills, experience, and other dimensions thought to be necessary to successful job performance. The candidate specification is normally prepared by the hiring manager, with occasional assistance provided by other department managers and/or the human resources department.

When well-prepared and carefully thought out, this specification can be a very valuable document. It frequently serves as the focal point for the employer's entire interview strategy. Advance knowledge of the contents of the document could prove equally as valuable to the interviewee, since it could be used as the basis for formulating an effective counterstrategy. Since this is not a practical consideration, the candidate must go through the same process as the employer in attempting to construct this specification.

When preparing the candidate specification, most hiring managers will review such things as the position description, current year's objectives, business plans, and so on. In essence, the manager is reviewing the general responsibilities of the position in an effort to determine the kind of person needed to meet these requirements. Such review typically results in a candidate specification that includes the following general categories: (1) education, (2) knowledge, (3) experience, (4) skills, and (5) personal attributes.

A typical candidate specification would probably read as follows:

Education. BS degree in mechanical engineering preferred; degree in chemical engineering acceptable.

Knowledge. Paper machine project engineering; wet end sheet formation.

Experience. Two plus years in design, installation, and start-up of tissue and/or towel machines; twin wire-forming machine experience helpful.

Skills. Solid engineering skills in mechanical design; project leadership of contractor personnel.

Personal Attributes: Intelligent, articulate; able to work effectively in fast-paced construction/start-up environment; willing to work long hours, including frequent evenings and weekends; willing to travel at least 40 percent of the time, including weekend travel.

Although admittedly a fairly abbreviated description, this candidate specification is very similar to those used by most organizations.

The employer's strategy now becomes one of interviewing to determine how well the prospective candidate meets this specification. In my example, some of the candidate's qualifications for the position will be evident from a quick review of the applicant's resume. However, such areas as "level of engineering knowledge" and "level of intelligence" cannot be measured by using the applicant's resume. These can only be ascertained through the interview process.

Interviewee Strategy

Considering the employer's interview strategy, as defined earlier in this chapter, how can the interviewee formulate a meaningful counterstrategy? What steps can the interviewee take to maximize the potential for a favorable interview outcome?

There are a number of things you can do to duplicate fairly accurately the employer's thinking process, thereby allowing yourself to plan an effective counterstrategy that will allow you to "stack the deck" in your favor. Here are some of them:

Advance Information

You will want to obtain as much information as possible about the position, prior to the actual interview. Although much of this information is readily available just for the asking, it has always amazed me how few employment candidates ever bother to request it.

Don't be shy about requesting this information since many employers are willing to provide it to you if it is available. The strategic advantage of acquiring this information in advance of the interview far outweighs the risks of an employer politely declining your request.

Where available without too much difficulty, you should request the following in advance of your visit:

1. Position job description.
2. Job objectives—current year.
3. Department objectives—current year.
4. Departmental or functional business plan.
5. Annual report.

CANDIDATE SPECIFICATION

During your initial telephone conversation with the employer, you should make it a point to ask for a verbal description of the kind of person they are seeking. Ask the employer to tell you not only what qualifications they are seeking, but also, which of these qualifications they consider to be the most important. If time allows, and you can avoid sounding pushy, ask why these factors are considered to be important.

If the employer begins to balk, suggest that you need this information to determine whether or not you are interested in the position and whether you feel you have sufficient qualifications to warrant investing your time in further discussions. This should seem a reasonable request at this stage of the relationship and you will usually get what you want.

It is best to request answers to these questions at the beginning of your discussions, since you will lose considerable leverage once the employer has ascertained that you are interested in the position and are prepared to go to the next step.

POSITION ANALYSIS

As with the employer, one of your first steps in formulating your interview strategy is to conduct an analysis of the position for which you will be interviewing. This procedure is similar to the employers' when they form the candidate specification. You will need to review the key responsibilities of the position in an effort to translate these into probable candidate selection criteria. The advance documents that you have collected from the employer should prove very helpful at this point.

The following set of questions should help you to walk through this process in a logical and thorough fashion. Space is provided for you to fill in your answers as you go along.

1. What are the *key ongoing responsibilities* of this position? (Job description should prove helpful here.) _____
   _____
   _____
   _____
   _____
   _____

2. What are the *key technical problems* to be solved, and *challenges* to be met, in satisfying these ongoing responsibilities?
   _____
   _____
   _____
   _____

3. What *technical* and/or *professional knowledge* does this suggest that a person must have in order to successfully solve these problems and meet these challenges? _____
   _____
   _____
   _____

4. What are the *specific objectives* for this position for the *current year?* _____
   _____
   _____
   _____

5. What are the *key technical challenges* that must be met and *problems* that must be solved if these objectives are to be successfully achieved? _____

_____

_____

_____

6. What *technical* and/or *professional knowledge* does this suggest that a person must have in order to successfully solve these problems and accomplish these objectives? _____

_____

_____

_____

_____

COMBINED CANDIDATE SPECIFICATION

You now have two sources from which to construct a candidate specification. The first is the initial telephone conversation with the prospective employer, and the second is the position analysis that you have just completed.

Chances are, if you have done a particularly thorough job with your position analysis, you may well have given more thought to the qualifications necessary to successful job performance than has the employer with whom you will be interviewing. This could serve to place you at a decided strategic advantage during the interview, allowing you to highlight important aspects of your background that are critical to achievement of desired organizational results.

Be careful not to get carried away with your newfound power, however, since this could serve to alienate the interviewer and cause you to be labeled as a show-off or "know-it-all."

Now, pause for a moment to review the overall candidate requirements as defined by both you and the employer. With these requirements in mind, use the following set of questions to help

75

you to translate these overall requirements into a combined candidate specification.

1. *Formal Education:* Considering the technical challenges of this position and the knowledge required, what formal education/training should the ideal candidate have (degree level and major)? Why? _____
   _____
   _____
   _____
   _____

2. *Training:* What informal education (training courses, seminars, etc.) would likely provide the required knowledge?
   _____
   _____
   _____
   _____

3. *Experience:* What level (number of years) and kind of experience would likely yield the depth and breadth of knowledge necessary for successful performance in this position?
   _____
   _____
   _____
   _____

4. *Related Experience:* What related or similar kinds of experience might yield the same kind of knowledge, and would therefore be an acceptable alternative? _____
   _____
   _____
   _____

5. *Skills:* What specific skills are required by the position, and how might these be acquired? _____

_____

_____

_____

_____

6. *Personal Attributes:* What personal attributes and characteristics are probably important for successful performance of this position? _____

_____

_____

_____

_____

COMPARATIVE ANALYSIS

The final step in preparing a traditional or common interview strategy is comparative analysis. You need to compare your own qualifications with those provided in the combined candidate specification which you have just developed. There is a great deal of logic to this step, since it is precisely what the interviewer will be doing both during and following the interview discussion. The interviewer will be comparing your qualifications with those contained in the employer's candidate specification. Forcing yourself to make the same kind of comparison will provide you with considerable insight into both your strengths and weaknesses and prepare you better for the interview discussion.

Start by reviewing the candidate specification to determine where your strengths lie. Note the specific areas where you meet and/or exceed the employer's requirements. In addition to listing specific educational and training qualifications (which are fairly self-evident and require little explanation), you will need to devote some time to developing a description of relevant work experience that you have had which could qualify you to successfully handle the position for which you will be interviewing. Here are some key questions to help you to define these areas:

1. What *functional knowledge* does this position require (marketing, sales, procurement, manufacturing, distribution, engineering, accounting, finance, human resources, etc.)?

2. In which of these functional areas have you had experience? What was the nature of that experience?

3. What is the *scope* of this position (budget, volumes, number of functions managed, number of people, etc.)?

4. What positions have you held that are similar in size, scope, and organizational complexity to this position?

5. What was the scope of these positions? Provide a quantitative description.

6. What key *technical problems* need to be solved in this position?

7. What similar technical problems have you solved? How did you solve them? What was the end result?

8. What specific training, education and/or experience has equipped you to solve these problems?

9. What unique ideas or creative approaches do you have for dealing with these key problems?

10. What are the key *managerial* challenges of this job?

11. What similar managerial challenges have you successfully met in the past? How did you meet these, and what were the results?

12. What unique or creative approaches do you have for addressing these key managerial problems?

13. What *personal characteristics* are essential for good job performance in this position?

14. In which of these personal dimensions do you excel? Cite examples of how these characteristics have complemented your performance.

15. Where are the *opportunities* to bring about major improvement to the function (i.e., increased productivity, improve quality, reduced costs)?

16. What unique qualifications do you possess that will enable you to lead such improvement?

You will not be able to answer some of these questions through comparative analysis alone. The advance documents that you have collected (job description, position objectives, business plan, etc.) will provide you with many clues. By utilizing these, you will be able to define many of the key issues and challenges faced by the employer.

Remember that the basis for modern interview theory states that the best single predictor of future job success is past job success. Employers will, therefore, be looking for evidence of successful past performance in areas of key interest. Therefore, be ready to give several examples of specific accomplishments in these key areas.

Although it is not my intent to focus on the negative, you must be prepared to address your weaknesses and shortcomings as well. Here again, by using comparative analysis and comparing your qualifications to the combined candidate specification, your weaknesses or shortcomings should be fairly evident. Rest assured that a seasoned interviewer will skillfully use such comparative analysis to uncover your failings, so you should be prepared to address them as well.

The following questions should prove helpful in developing a strategy for addressing these shortcomings during the interview. These will hopefully serve to help you to minimize the damage:

1. In which key areas are you either underqualified or unqualified?
2. How critical are these areas to successful job performance?
3. Specifically, in what ways are you lacking (education, training, experience, etc.)?
4. Do you have sufficient related qualifications (education, training, experience, etc.) that are transferable?
5. Can these areas be learned (through education, training, experience) on the job without seriously jeopardizing job performance?
6. What kind of program could you suggest to remedy these shortcomings?

There is little to be gained by misstating or overstating your qualifications during the employment interview. This is especially true if the area being probed is absolutely critical to successful job performance. Although you may win the battle, you're sure to lose the war! You may win the job offer, but your ensuing performance may well cost you an otherwise successful and prosperous career. Getting a single job offer is just not that important when your entire career is at stake.

By completing this comparative analysis and answering the questions that I have posed, you should be exceptionally well prepared to handle the traditional or common employment interview. This exercise should have automatically resulted in the development of a highly effective basic interview strategy that is geared to those areas that will be of interest to the employer. I have seen this type of strategy work very effectively time and time again. Over the years, it has proven to be highly successful in winning job offers.

7

The Five-Minute Concept

For several months prior to writing this book, I spent some time thinking about the hundreds of interviews that I have conducted over the years as an employment professional. My objective was to recall those occasional interviews where the candidate was unusually effective and stood out from the pack, so to speak. I recall some of these quite well.

These were the interviews where the candidate was so impressive that, before half of the interview schedule had been completed, the hiring manager was calling to implore me to hire the person. Such conversations usually went something like this:

> I just finished interviewing Joan, and she is an outstanding candidate! What do we need to do to get her? I want to make sure that we make her an offer before she leaves today. I want to pull out all the stops on this one!

What was going on in such interviews that made the candidate seem so outstanding? In what manner were these interviews different from the hundreds of other interviews of which I have been a part? Was there something different or unique about the candidate's approach that accounted for such an overwhelmingly positive impact? What valuable lessons could an inexperienced candidate, or highly seasoned veteran for that matter, learn from such dramatically positive interview cases?

These were the questions I pondered as I reviewed these highly successful interviews. My purpose was to identify those interview techniques that consistently produced job offers.

In addition to my personal observations, I informally discussed the subject with a few other experienced employment professionals as well. I wanted to see whether or not there were any uniform observations and conclusions that could be drawn about highly effective interviewing techniques.

At first glance, the answers to my questions seemed very apparent. Simply put, those who are highly successful interviewees are simply better qualified than their counterparts. Required knowledge and skills are solidly in place, and these candidates seem exceptionally well-motivated. The "personal chemistry" factors are also present, and it appears that the candidates would fit in well with their immediate work group. Additionally, these candidates posses good verbal communications skills and are very effective at describing their qualifications for the position.

Having made these preliminary observations, I couldn't help asking, "Is this all there is to it? Are these truly the only factors that account for interview success? If one answers yes and accepts this premise, then we can only conclude that, assuming basic requisite skills and knowledge, success in the employment interview process can be achieved simply by improving one's personal style and communications techniques.

Although there is something to be said for improvement in both of these areas, this kind of narrow thinking suggests that there is little the candidate can do in the strategic sense to affect the outcome of the employment interview. Instinctively, as a seasoned employment veteran, I can tell you that this is definitely not the case. Interview strategy can, and *does*, have a very significant impact on interview results.

Perhaps the greatest impetus toward my thinking more deeply on this subject was provided by the very sobering, and initially surprising, realization that not all of the employment candidates who have caused so much excitement about their candidacies have possessed all of the requisite knowledge and skills required by the employer. Surprisingly, as I think back over these interviews, I can recall several instances where the candidates had, in fact, only moderate or even marginal qualifications for the job.

Thinking further about this subject, I became increasingly convinced that interview success is not solely related to candidate qualifications. Instead, there seems to be plenty of hard evidence to support the contention that what a candidate "does" during the employment interview is just as important, if not more important, than what he or she "knows." Supporting this belief is the fact that some candidates who clearly had superior technical qualifications have not always been the ones to be hired. In fact, I have seen numerous cases where those who have had outstanding qualifications but interviewed poorly were at a decided competitive disadvantage when contrasted with their less qualified counterparts with good interview skills.

Further, I have personally witnessed cases where a particularly powerful interview strategy, coupled with a convincing presentation by the candidate, has actually caused the employer to change the original requirements, and even content of a position, to fit what was felt to be a particularly attractive candidate.

Thus, having a well-planned interview strategy has the potential to substantially improve your results and provide you with a significant competitive advantage!

One such interview strategy is the "five-minute interview." This is a potentially powerful interview strategy that has been applied time and time again by employment candidates, very often with positive results. If carefully planned and well executed, it unquestionably has the potential to be one of the most powerful and dynamic tools that you can utilize to positively affect the outcome of your employment interviews. Perhaps more than any other interview technique, the five-minute interview strategy has repeatedly accounted for a consistently high number of job offers.

This chapter is devoted to exploring the basic principles that underlie the five-minute interview concept. It is intended to provide you with sufficient understanding of these principles to convince you of its value as an interview technique and to help you to feel comfortable in adapting it as a major part of your overall interview strategy.

In order for you to appreciate more fully the importance of the five-minute interview strategy and its potential effectiveness, it is important that we first contrast it with the traditional approach to interviewing. Having made this comparison, we will then discuss the steps you will need to take in order to adopt and utilize this five-minute strategy as an important element of your interview process.

THE MAINTENANCE INTERVIEW

In order that you might better appreciate the significance and value of the five-minute interview approach as an interview strategy, it is important to compare it to the interview strategy most frequently used by employment candidates. This traditional strategy is what I call the *maintenance approach.*

Usually when approaching the job interview, most candidates tend to focus on the job "as it now exists." Interestingly, this is true of the employer as well. There is a general tendency for both to think of the job as being somewhat static or nonchanging—as if somehow frozen in time. The tendency is to think about the position as it is currently defined and as performed by its present occupant.

It is rare that much, if any, thought is given by either party as to how the job "might" be performed. There is thus what we might call a "status quo" mentality. Let's examine this maintenance concept more closely to get a better understanding of what is occurring in this traditional approach to interviewing.

Think of the steps that the employer normally goes through in preparing for an interview. I am sure that most of you are familiar with this process, and likely have gone through it yourself at one time or another.

First, the employer will usually pull a copy of the job description from the files. If no description exists, one may need to be developed. Second, the employer will then review this description to define the key responsibilities of the position. These responsibilities are then reviewed to determine the qualifications needed for good job performance.

As an additional step, the employer may, if reasonably conscientious, review the performance of current and past holders of the position to see if their respective performances, either singularly or as a group, will yield some clues as to which qualifications are key to successful job performance. The resulting qualifications derived from this process then become the candidate specification against which all prospective job applicants will be measured to determine their suitability for employment.

On the other side of the employment equation, one of the first things that the employment candidate usually does is to secure, either verbally or in written form, the same position description. This is important to the candidate for purposes of determining job interest, but it is also necessary when preparing an appropriate interview strategy as well. By ascertaining the key responsibilities of the position, the candidate can then make some attempt to predict (accurately or not) what the employer will be seeking in the way of candidate qualifications (the hiring profile). This profile then serves as a sort of mental road map which the interviewee follows during the employment process, mentioning specific qualifications thought to be of interest to the employer as the opportunity presents itself.

The important observation that should be made here is that both the candidate and the employer go through a strikingly similar thought process when preparing for the interview discussion. Invariably, the bulk of the focus for both parties is on the existing position and current job accountabilities. Little thought is given to the future requirements of the position.

There is nothing fundamentally wrong with the maintenance approach to interviewing. It continues to provide a solid, logical basis for the development of basic interview strategy, and will, I am sure, continue to win employment offers if well planned and executed by the employment candidate. Since the maintenance approach is the most commonly used approach to interviewing, however, there is no particular competitive advantage to be gained by adopting it as your primary strategy. Unless you have unusual skills and knowledge, to do so will serve simply to lump you with all the hundreds of other candidates that pass through the employer's doors.

This is not to say that the maintenance approach should not be used. To the contrary, as we have already shown in Chapter 6, "Basic Interview Strategy," it is a useful approach and will serve to strengthen your interview effectiveness. However, you will need to adopt a broader and more convincing strategy if you wish to set yourself apart from the competition and cause some genuine excitement about your employment candidacy.

THE GREAT CULTURAL CHANGE

Today, there is more reason than ever to question the wisdom of relying on conventional interview strategy. There are some very

powerful economic and social forces presently at work that are beginning to revolutionize the overall employment selection and interview process. As an interviewee, you need to be keenly aware
of these shifts since they could have far-reaching implications for
your employment interview strategy.

These forces are so powerful, and the resulting change so
rapid that they could potentially render conventional interview
strategy obsolete. It is certainly evident to me that this change is
already well underway, and, as an employment candidate, you
need to be very aware of it.

Let's take some time at this point to examine more closely
the sweeping nature and extent of this change.

Today, perhaps more than any other time in the history of
this country, American industry and organizations are undergoing
a significant cultural change. You needn't look much further than
a current edition of the *Wall Street Journal* or *BusinessWeek* for
undeniable evidence of this phenomenon.

Intense global and domestic competition has forced many
American companies into a survival mode. Cheap labor and ma-
terial costs, coupled in some cases with superior quality and/or
functionality, have given many foreign companies a decided competitive advantage in the American marketplace. The current
American foreign trade deficit serves as a clear barometer of the
severity of this problem.

This intense competition is forcing major cultural change
within the industrial community as never before. To meet this
fierce competition, American concerns are actively focusing on all
facets of their operations in an effort to discover and bring about
major improvements in overall productivity, quality, and costs.

The private sector is not alone in its quest for excellence.
The public sector is also undergoing major change. Here the

competition, no less fierce than that faced by American industry, is for funding. The political pressures for reduced taxes and a balanced budget are now forcing many governmental agencies, and the various nonprofit organizations which they support, to undergo enormous cultural change. As with industry, these organizations are frantically looking for ways to reduce costs and substantially increase employee productivity.

EMPLOYEE PRODUCTIVITY

As part of an overall plan to restore competitive health, the emphasis of most organizations is on doing more with fewer people.

For most organizations, the first step toward achieving this objective has been to go through what has come to be known as the "skinnying down" process. We've all read about the various creative packages offered by so many companies to older workers in an effort to induce them to retire early. There have also been the "open door" programs aimed at reducing the ranks of younger workers by offering financial inducements for voluntary termination.

Additionally, as we are all very much aware, there have been a great number of organizations that have already implemented large employee cutbacks and layoffs. Many employers have carried out cutbacks in the range of 10, 20, 30, 40, and even 50 percent. This is not to mention those companies that have recently sold or shut down entire operations.

On the other side of the coin, employers are looking for ways to increase the output of those workers remaining in the organization after the skinnying down process is complete. These efforts usually fall under the banner of organization effectiveness, a rapidly emerging business function aimed at unleashing the untapped potential of employees at all organizational levels.

Substantially increasing numbers of companies have plunged headlong into a wide range of participatory management programs (e.g., the Japanese quality circles, Krone's management process, Deming's statistical process control) aimed at greatly increasing employee productivity through increased participation in the management process. By creating a sense of increased ownership, it is believed that employees who participate in these kinds of programs see themselves as stakeholders in the ultimate success of the enterprise and are, therefore, increasingly motivated to use a greater portion of their total capability to achieve the overall goals of the organization.

This strong desire for increased employee productivity and improved organizational effectiveness is what accounted for the enormous success of publications such as Peters and Waterman's book, *In Search of Excellence*. American business and institutional leaders currently have an enormous appetite for organizational and cultural changes that will restore their enterprises to competitive health and market preeminence. And, they are looking for people to lead this change!

Changes in compensation systems are also rapidly beginning to reflect an organizational desire for increased productivity. Companies are looking for creative ways to link individual and group compensation to increased productivity and profitability as never before. This has resulted in a fast-growing trend of shifting the emphasis from "fixed" forms of compensation (i.e., annual salaries and hourly wage rates) to "incentive" forms of compensation (i.e., bonuses, profit sharing) that are directly tied to organizational productivity and profitability objectives.

CHANGE AGENTS

These massive cultural and organizational changes now fully reflect themselves in a major way in the employment interview and selection process. Such changes have had the effect of totally revolutionizing the traditional candidate profile sought by most employers, thus rendering traditional interview strategy all but obsolete.

In some cases, the traditional approach to interviewing has already caused employment candidates to fall far short of employer requirements. We have seen a dramatic drop in demand for candidates whose focus is on maintaining the status quo (i.e., simply performing the existing job). There has been a corresponding increase in demand for individuals who will be "change agents"—those who openly challenge the traditional ways of doing things, and who continuously seek new and better ways!

Thus, those who are keepers of the status quo are on the way out, and those who are the leaders of change are on the way in. This has important implications for candidate interview strategy.

Interviewees need to be keenly aware of this shifting focus, and they will need to make corresponding adjustments to their interview approach if they truly wish to be the recipient of job offers. Yes, employers seem to be becoming increasingly turned off by the traditional interview strategy that is simply aimed at convincing them that you can "perform the job." Instead, they are becoming increasingly drawn to those who demonstrate they can bring positive change and increased value to the organization.

Thus, there has been a shift away from current job performance capability as the key criteria for employee selection and a decided swing toward the candidate's ability to help the organization move forward in its quest to reach its strategic goals and objectives. Most organizations feel that they need change agents if they are to survive and grow in today's increasingly competitive environment. They need creative, motivated people who will bring major change and add significant new capability and value to their enterprises.

Highly successful interviewees understand this "value-added" concept. They understand the importance of selling employers on their ability to bring change and improvement to the organization. They have been particularly successful at positioning themselves as positive change agents. What is different, however, is that the nature of todays' fiercely competitive marketplace places much greater value on such capability with a significant premium being attached to this change capability by the entire employment community.

It should be clear, then, that you will need an interview strategy that is much broader than the traditional approach if you expect to be successful in your interviews and general employment campaign. You will need to focus beyond the current job requirements and build an interview strategy that is geared toward achievement of the organization's strategic goals and objectives. This strategy should position you as an organization change agent—one who can lead organization change and add value to the company. This principle is at the very core of the five-minute interview concept.

EMPLOYER "HOT BUTTONS"

Posturing yourself as a change agent who can add value to the organization is not in itself an absolute guarantee of successful interview results. It is essential that such change be seen by the organization as truly important to business objectives and strategic aims. You must first understand what it is that the employer wishes to achieve before you can design an interview strategy that will truly command his or her attention and whet the desire to hire you.

Lack of such employer understanding can quickly cause an otherwise effective and well-planned strategy to go awry. Areas that you consider to represent great opportunity for organizational change and improvement may, in fact, be areas in which the organization has little or no interest in changing. To extoll your virtues and capabilities as a change agent in these areas could have an adverse effect on your interview effectiveness. At best you will likely bore your interviewer to death, and at worst you may destroy your employment chances! Thus, you must understand what is truly important to the employer if you are going to have a meaningful impact. You must know what areas the organization feels need fixing.

There is a famous sales adage that says, "Sell the sizzle and not the steak." In order to be successful at sales, you must first determine what will motivate your prospect to buy. Having determined these motivational factors, you can then better package the characteristics of your product to match your customer's needs and thus substantially increase the probability of a successful sale. Interviewing is no different. You must know what will motivate the employer to hire you, and you must package and sell your skills and capabilities accordingly. These motivational factors are known as the employer's "hot buttons."

Top sales persons have always understood the importance of hot buttons. They have also understood that what motivates one person to buy may have little or no effect on another. Each may have entirely different motivational factors. What's more, a given buyer's motivational factors may change with the passage of time. What was important last month, what would have motivated the individual to buy, may not currently apply. Two months ago price may have been important, last month, quality, and this month service. If the salesperson is inattentive to these changes, he or she may attempt to sell the wrong factors and the net result is simple—no sale! As an interviewee, if you are not aware of these differences in employer motivational factors, the net result will be just as simple—no employment offer!

Therefore, as with the sales representative, in order to interview effectively, you must start by gaining insight into what will motivate the employer. Ask yourself the following questions:

1. Where is the employer headed?
2. What organizational goals and objectives are of greatest importance?

You must start by defining the employer's hot buttons, those things that will motivate the employer to hire you. As you will see, the five-minute interview is designed to do just that. It is designed to help you to define the employer's hot buttons and then to build a total interview strategy that focuses on the strategic needs of the organization. This strategy plays to those very things that will motivate employers and compel them to make an offer.

FIRST IMPRESSIONS DON'T DO IT

Somewhere you have probably been told that the employment interview is frequently won or lost during the first 30 seconds. Don't believe it.

Students of this concept have gone to great lengths to make their point. Reasons given for this 30-second phenomenon are frequently based on the argument that the interviewer's first impressions are the most powerful and are, therefore, the most difficult to change.

Much has been written to stress the importance of first impressions on the final outcome of the interview process. These pieces usually dwell on the importance of such factors as neat appearance, firm handshake, good eye contact, pleasant demeanor, proper body language, and so on.

Although I cannot dispute the importance of having these hygienic factors in place in order to get the interview off to a good start, I feel that the importance of these factors is frequently blown out of proportion in the context of the overall interview and employment process. Most of today's professional interviewers are simply too sophisticated to allow these surface issues to dominate the hiring decision.

So that I am not labeled a heretic and threatened with expulsion from the professional interviewer corps, however, let me make it perfectly clear that I have *not* said that first impressions are unimportant to the interview process. This is not my point at all. To the contrary, I believe that first impressions *are* important and that they *do* influence the outcome of the employment interview. The key word here, however, is "influence." Although I believe that hygienic factors can (and do) *influence* interview results, I do not believe that they *determine* such results. Today's employers have substantially more important things on their minds than a nice smile or a firm handshake! Paramount among these are such things as organizational survival, competitive intercept (the process of tracking your competition in order to determine the direction and speed of their strategy), organization effectiveness, employee productivity, strategic mission, and so on.

As an executive of a major international search firm, I am seeing an increasing preoccupation with these kinds of concerns.

In my discussions with client companies, more and more frequently I hear such words as "cultural change," "strategic objectives," "value added," "change agent," "organizational excellence," and so on.

In increasing numbers, employers appear to be looking for ways to improve their hiring results through improved interviewing and selection techniques that are more closely tied to organizational results. There appears to be a greater understanding and appreciation for the relationship between good employee selection and organizational productivity. Employers, for the most part, are looking more and more to the interview and selection process as a key opportunity through which to enhance employee productivity and positively affect bottom line results.

With this renewed emphasis on results, it appears that some of these first impression factors are playing a lesser role in the overall selection process. I fully expect this trend to continue as employers become increasingly adept at the use of penetrating interview techniques aimed at real productivity factors.

THE FIRST FIVE MINUTES

The early part of the interview is extremely important for a reason that goes far beyond simply making a favorable impression on the interviewer. It is important, for some entirely different reasons, that candidates make excellent use of the first five minutes of the interview, during which they can acquire some very significant information. It is this information on which the interviewee can forge an interview strategy that is designed to win. This information relates to organizational strategy—the strategic goals and objectives of the organization.

Without knowledge of where the organization is headed and what new challenges will need to be faced, it will be impossible to design an interview strategy that positions one as a change agent. Where is the organization headed? What changes does it wish to bring about? Which changes are important? These and similar questions must first be answered before one can formulate a convincing and compelling interview approach.

Without answers to these questions early in the interview discussion (preferably within the first five minutes), you will be like a rudderless ship adrift in a storm. You will be totally at the mercy of the interviewer and will be buffeted and pushed in many directions with no idea of your direction or final destination. It is far better that you secure your bearings up front, and that you have sufficient time to plan an effective strategy that will provide you with some self-confidence and a sense of direction, purpose, and control.

In Chapter 8, "The Five-Minute Interview," I will help you to develop some techniques that should assist you in securing this important strategic information about the employer early in the interview.

8

The Five-Minute
Interview

In the preceding chapter, we established a strong case for the five-minute interview strategy as a powerful technique for use by the interviewee in winning job offers. If well-planned and executed, it can serve to create considerable interest and excitement about your employment candidacy, since it serves to position you as a change agent who has the capability to bring improvement and add value to the hiring organization.

As discussed, the reason for the success of this particular strategy is that it focuses on those things that are of paramount importance to the employer—those things that the employer perceives to be important to the achievement of the organization's long-term strategic goals. What we didn't discuss, however, is how to define these strategic goals and objectives. In particular, how does one define these important factors during the first five minutes of the employment interview? This is the subject of this chapter.

Perhaps, to gain some insight into those techniques that might be used to ferret out this vital information, it might prove helpful to observe two different types of interviews. The first will be the traditional interview approach and will focus on the existing position as it is currently performed. The second, five-minute interview, will focus on the strategic goals and objectives of the hiring organization. By contrasting these two approaches, you will acquire a greater appreciation for the strategic approach, and will also have an opportunity to observe some of the interview questions and techniques that can be used by the interviewee to both define and focus on the organization's goals and objectives.

SAMPLE TRADITIONAL INTERVIEW

Employer: Good morning Mr. Jones. How was your trip?

Candidate: Good morning Ms. Bates. My trip was fine, thanks to your excellent directions. It only took me 45 minutes and, as you had predicted, there was very little traffic.

Employer: I'm glad you had a good trip. Please have a seat.

Candidate: Thank you.

Employer: Mr. Jones, as you know, we will be talking to you about a position in our human resources department as the manager of organizational effectiveness. This position reports to the director of human resources and will have responsibility for handling training and development as well as the organizational effectiveness functions. Reporting to this position are the training and development manager, the department secretary, and two administrative assistants.

Candidate: Sounds very interesting!

Employer: Yes, it is a very interesting and challenging assignment.

Mr. Jones, we hope to use today's interview to get to know you well and to provide you with a lot of information about us as well. We will want to discuss your educational background, your training, your work experience, your accomplishments, your work style and management philosophy. In this way, we will get to know you well and have the kind of information which we feel will be of most importance to making a good employment decision for both you and the Parker Company. Our employment philosophy here at Parker is that it is either a good two-way fit, or it's not a fit at all.

It is also important that you have an opportunity to ask questions. The more you know about the Parker Company, the better prepared you will be to make a good decision.

Well now, why don't we get started. Tell me about your educational background. Where did you go to school?

Candidate: I went to the University of Michigan for my undergraduate training and to Michigan State for my master's.

Employer: Michigan State has an excellent graduate program in human resources. What did you think of the curriculum?

Candidate: I felt it was an excellent program and was pleased that I had decided to go there.

Employer: What courses did you enjoy the most?

Candidate: I particularly enjoyed the courses I took in organization design and human resources planning. Another favorite was the course I took in open systems planning.

Employer: Tell me Mr. Jones, what kind of a student were you?

Candidate: As an undergraduate, I was a fairly serious student. I was conscientious and worked hard. My overall grade point average was 3.2 on a 4.0 scale—good enough to land a partial scholarship to graduate school at Michigan State.

Employer: Very interesting. It sounds as if you did very well.

Now, let's spend some time discussing your work experience. Since our time is somewhat limited, I would like to focus on the last two positions that you held with the Bollinger Corporation: personnel manager for the art supplies division and corporate training manager. Tell me about your position as personnel manager. Who did you report to, and what were your major responsibilities?

Candidate: As personnel manager of the art supplies division, I reported directly to the general manager of the division. My major responsibilities included internal and external staffing, wage and salary administration, benefits administration, training and development, performance and potential administration, medical, safety, and security.

Employer: That sounds like a rather broadly scoped assignment. Tell me, what kind of support did you have? What did your organization look like and what kind of budget did you have?

Candidate: I managed a department of six people. Reporting directly to me were the salary and benefits manager, the manager of safety and security and a training specialist. Indirectly reporting was a clerical staff of three support personnel. My annual budget was approximately $2.5 million.

Employer: Mr. Jones, what do you consider to be your major accomplishments while in the position of personnel manager of the art supplies division? Of which of these achievement are you most proud, and why?

Candidate: Let's see, there were several major accomplishments. There was the new performance evaluation system that we designed in-house, the installation and startup of the Hay job evaluation system, and a training survey to better define the division's training and development needs. I suppose the new evaluation system had the most favorable impact on the division, and, as such, was my most significant accomplishment.

Employer: Why is that?

Candidate: Well, the old system was felt to be very lopsided and unfair. It was causing a serious morale problem throughout the division. The old system provided for input from only one source, the immediate supervisor. Under the new system, there is input not only from the supervisor, but from individual employees and their peer group as well.

Employer: And this proved to be a better system?

Candidate: Yes, employees felt they were treated much better as a result of this change. The system provided for far more objective evaluations and caused a big upswing in division morale.

Employer: Are there any other major accomplishments of which you are particularly proud? If so, what are they?

Candidate: Well, as I already mentioned, I installed and initiated the Hay job evaluation system. I also helped develop the division training survey. However, I suppose that neither of these had the same degree of impact as the performance evaluation system.

Employer: Why don't we move on to your position as corporate training manager. Tell me, how did you come to be selected for this position? Was this a promotion for you?

Candidate: Yes, this was a promotion to the corporate human resources staff and entailed a move to corporate headquarters in Philadelphia. I was told that I had been identified for this position as the result of a company-wide search. In addition, I have maintained high performance evaluations and had, on more than one occasion, told the director of corporate personnel that I had a strong interest in an assignment in the corporate training function.

Employer: A strong interest in the corporate training function?

Candidate: Yes, my interest in training and development stems from my belief that of all the human resources functions, training has the greatest potential for making a major contribution to the bottom line of a business enterprise.

Employer: Really, why do you feel this way?

Candidate: Because training has the potential to increase the overall capability of the organization by adding knowledge and skills to the organizational mix. Only through the addition of new capability can the organization bring about change and improvement to business results.

Employer: But isn't that the role of organizational effectiveness and organizational development? Aren't these functions charged with the responsibility for bringing about organizational change?

Candidate: Well, I suppose so, but I still believe that the most meaningful and lasting changes can come from training. After all, the entire basis for training and development is behavior modification and, without change in behavior, there can be no organizational change and improvement.

Employer: An interesting theory, but what about the role of organizational effectiveness? Today, there seems to be a mad scramble by a number of companies to use new employee involvement and participatory management approaches. Isn't this trend aimed at bringing about cultural change and organizational improvement through greater employee involvement and productivity?

Candidate: I suppose you're right about that, but I question whether such programs can really have the kind of lasting impact that a well-planned and well-executed training strategy can have on the organization.

Employer: Well, as you know, Mr. Jones, we are talking about a position as manager of organization effectiveness here at

Parker. I'd be curious as to how you would approach this position. What would be your strategy for managing this function effectively?

Candidate: I'm not sure what you mean. Do you mean, how would I manage the people?

Employer: Well, that's part of it, but I'm more interested in your overall approach or strategy for managing the function. What do you believe the role of an organizational effectiveness manager should be, and how would you go about implementing this role in the organization?

Candidate: Wow, that's a tough one! Let me see. I guess I would start by conducting a survey to determine the training needs of the business. After all, satisfying these needs will develop the capability of people to bring about the change needed to reach the goals of the organization. I would then define the training programs that will best satisfy these needs. I suppose that this would be my overall approach or functional strategy. What do you think?

Employer: Well, that's an interesting approach, but unfortunately we've just run out of time and we're going to need to move you on to your next appointment. I really appreciate your coming in to talk with us today. Thank you very much. We'll be back to you shortly.

Candidate: Thank you. I've enjoyed meeting you as well.

As you could see, the interviewee was in trouble in this interview almost from the start. To begin with, there was no attempt made by the candidate to determine what was really important to the employer. The interviewee was too busy attempting to convince the employer of the importance of the training function to take the necessary time needed to qualify the interests of the employer. It didn't become clear until the later stages of the discussion that the employer had a stronger interest in organizational effectiveness than in the value of training to the organization. By this time in the discussion, it was already too late for the interviewee to change strategy.

Importantly, there was no attempt made by the interviewee to gain an understanding of the strategic direction and objectives of either the corporation or the human resources function. This was also a major flaw in this candidate's interview strategy.

Without these important guideposts at the beginning of the interview discussion, the candidate was completely at the mercy of the interviewer. The interviewee was off balance during much of the discussion and was all but powerless to significantly affect the outcome of the interview.

Now let's examine a much different kind of interview. In this example, the interviewee will make effective use of the five-minute interview strategy. Note in particular the various techniques used by the interviewee during the first few minutes of discussion to define the aspects of the position considered to be most important to the employer. Note also the candidate's efforts to gain some insight into the strategic goals of the company. And, most Importantly, observe the overall improved performance of the interviewee as the result of applying the five-minute interview concept.

SAMPLE FIVE-MINUTE INTERVIEW

Employer: Good morning, Ms. Criswell. How was your flight in?

Candidate: It was relatively smooth; however, we were delayed for about an hour in Atlanta. Fortunately, I was able to arrive in time.

Employer: Well, I'm certainly glad you're here. Hopefully your return flight will go a little more smoothly.

Ms. Criswell, as you are aware, we will be talking to you about the position of manager of organizational effectiveness in our human resources department. This position reports to the corporate director of human resources and will have functional responsibility for training and development as well as organizational effectiveness. Reporting to this position are the training and development manager, the departmental secretary, and two administrative assistants.

Candidate: Sounds like an interesting position!

Employer: Yes, it should prove to be a very interesting and challenging assignment.

Candidate: Challenging? That's good. I've always liked challenging jobs. In what ways do you feel it will be challenging?

Employer: Well, organizational effectiveness is a new function for us here at Parker. Although many of us are not really sure what it is about, we know that it has the potential to bring about cultural change, which is something that our chairman of the board feels is important for us to do. But, I'm getting a little ahead of myself. Let's first spend some time talking about you.

Candidate: If you'll forgive the interruption, I feel it's interesting to know that your chairman has a personal interest in the organizational effectiveness function. What is happening within this company to stimulate the chairman's interest? What does he hope to achieve by having an organizational effectiveness function?

Employer: Well, our overall performance as a company has slipped somewhat in the last five years or so. Now don't get me wrong, our sales volume has been growing, as our annual report will attest. In fact, sales last year were up nearly 20 percent over the previous year and sales so far this year appear fairly strong. The problem is market share. Fortunately, we are in a growing market, and this market growth has accounted for increased sales overall. However, our market share has fallen nearly five percentage points in the last year alone. Yearger is beginning to give us some very stiff competition.

Candidate: What form has this increased competition taken? Is it better price or quality? Is their product line a better one, or do they have better service? What are the key factors accounting for this slippage?

Employer: Well, the most important factor is that Yearger has introduced a broader product line and thus presents the customer with a broader selection from which to choose. There are also some variations in price. The net result is that the customer can usually select a Yearger product that is a closer match to the specific need and is also, in most cases, slightly cheaper than what we can offer.

Candidate: That's interesting! What's Parker's strategy? How are they going to counter this threat from Yearger? What organizational changes are they looking to bring about to accomplish this? Also, how do these immediate changes fit with Parker's long-term strategy?

Employer: Wow, that's a lot of questions. I'm not sure where to start.

Candidate: I'm sorry. Perhaps I did get a bit carried away. Maybe it would be easier to talk about short-term and long-term strategy separately. What is Parker's immediate strategy? What is the chairman looking to accomplish in the near future?

Employer: Short-term, our strategy is a defensive one. We need to increase our product line in order to compete with Yearger's line. There is a lot of pressure on research and development to roll out some new products to meet this objective. Second, we need to get our manufacturing and distribution costs down so that our pricing can be more competitive.

Candidate: Sounds like a worthwhile objective to me! How do you feel this objective impacts on the position of manager of organizational effectiveness? What new responsibilities and accountabilities will this position have that it does not have now? In general, what new results will be expected?

Employer: Well, as you may recall from our earlier discussion, we have not previously had an organizational effectiveness function as such. Up until now, I suppose that the responsibility for organizational effectiveness belonged to the manager of training and development.

Candidate: Oh, yes, I do recall that you said that it is a new position. Well, let me rephrase my question then. Considering the company's short-term strategy, what key results do you feel the company is looking for from this position? What are the expectations?

Employer: Well, up to this point in time the main focus of the training and development function has been on training. The current training and development manager, in fact, has done an excellent job of surveying the training needs of the business and developing the necessary programs needed to meet these needs. What is needed now is someone who can play a lead role in bringing about cultural change within the corporation. The chairman feels that, as an organization, we have become somewhat stagnant—that we are in somewhat of a rut. He feels we need someone who will force us to think differently, someone who will cause us to challenge the traditional ways of doing things, someone who will stimulate change and organizational improvement. He also feels that we need to reach out and involve employees in the business. We need to increase their commitment to the business and find ways to increase overall employee contribution and productivity.

Candidate: Well, I'm glad that we've had this conversation. Without it, I probably would have focused too much on my background in training. I suppose you're far more interested in knowing about my training and experience in organizational effectiveness. Aren't you?

Employer: Yes, that is the key area of interest.

Candidate: Would you like me to tell you about my formal training in organizational effectiveness?

Employer: Yes, that sounds like a good place to start. What training or formal education have you had in this area?

Candidate: Well, my formal education includes a number of related courses at both the graduate and undergraduate level.

Employer: What courses were these?

Candidate: I have had courses in organization planning, organization design, organization systems and processes, industrial psychology, intervention techniques, organization change dynamics, open systems planning, and quality circles. I have also attended several one-week seminars conducted by some of the leading experts in the field of organizational effectiveness. These have included the Krone leadership series and Deming's course in statistical process control. I am thus well-schooled in a broad range of organizational effectiveness concepts and techniques and can provide strong technical leadership in this area.

Employer: Yes, it does sound as if you've had some excellent training in this area. Now, let's discuss your work experience.

Candidate: I assume you will want me to focus on the experience that I have had in organization effectiveness. Right?

Employer: Right.

Candidate: Well, as you can see, my resume does a pretty thorough job of describing the various positions that I have held. Perhaps my most relevant experience, though, is when I was manager of organizational effectiveness at Dart. Perhaps this would be the best place to start.

Employer: Yes, that sounds like a good place to start.

Candidate: Well, when I first became manager of organization at Dart, the situation was not dissimilar from the situation currently being faced by Parker. They were in a bit of a rut. Morale was particularly low and productivity and market share were both slipping. Clearly something needed to be done to shake things up and to revitalize employee interest and commitment. I worked closely with the president of Dart, Walter Everett, to structure a plan that would bring the needed changes about. Using various organizational effectiveness techniques, I first worked with Everett's staff to identify what they considered to be the major issues and barriers standing in the way of achieving their corporate goals. Next, we identified those groups who had opportunity to make an impact. The net result of our effort was a 35 percent increase in sales coupled with a 25 percent improvement in market share. This was also accompanied by a 10 percent reduction in cost of goods manufactured.

Employer: An impressive accomplishment!

Candidate: Yes, I was very pleased with the results. We all worked very hard to get to this point. I am confident that with proper support from your chairman, similar results could be achieved here at Parker. I would very much like the opportunity to manage such a program here at Parker. I am confident that we could achieve some exciting results!

Employer: Yes, I agree. I'm anxious for you to meet our chairman. I'm sure he'll be very interested in hearing what you have to say. At this point, however, we've run out of time and I need to get you to your next appointment. I've enjoyed talking with you very much.

Candidate: Likewise, I've enjoyed talking with you. Thanks for meeting with me! I look forward to seeing you again.

Although it is difficult to portray a full and complete interview, I have hopefully given you enough to make it absolutely clear that there is a world of difference in the effect of these two interviews. The five-minute interview concept is a powerful tool when compared to the traditional interview approach. The key advantage is that the five-minute technique allows you to define what is important to the employer at the beginning of the discussion. This then allows you to plan an interview strategy that focuses on those areas of paramount importance to the interviewer, rather than to wander aimlessly through the interview, emphasizing areas that are of little or no real importance to the employer and the employment decision.

Since the five-minute interview focuses on the hiring organization's short- and long-term strategic objectives, it has the added benefit of allowing the interviewee to position him or herself as someone who can help to bring these desired changes about—someone who will add value to the organization beyond simply performing the existing job as it is now performed. It allows candidates to position themselves as employees who will be positive change agents and who can help the organization to realize its future goals.

Finally, knowing what the company considers to be important provides the interviewee with much greater self-confidence during the interview process. It allows the candidate to participate in the interview discussions in a far more meaningful way.

Instead of feeling like a rudderless ship left in a storm, the candidate is no longer helpless and at the mercy of the interviewer. Instead, there is a clear understanding of where the interview is headed, and why. This knowledge allows the interviewee a degree of comfort and control that would otherwise not be there. It places both the candidate and the interviewer on a more equal footing and neutralizes the flow of power. No longer is the interviewee subject to the absolute control of the interviewer. Instead, there is the opportunity for the candidate to carefully seize control of the discussions from time to time, and to focus on those things that might not otherwise come out in the course of the employer's normal line of inquiry.

It should be very clear to you by now that the candidate who uses the five-minute interview strategy has an enormous advantage over those who make use of the traditional approach to interviewing. Those who use the traditional approach are simply portraying themselves as people who can perform the current responsibilities of the job. On the other hand, those who employ the five-minute interview, with emphasis on the organization's future goals and strategy, will be perceived as individuals who are not just interested in today. They are perceived as persons who are focused on the future — persons who are committed to bringing about changes and improvements that will help the organization get to where it is going. These are the individuals who

are perceived to be in continuous pursuit of excellence and who will provide the organization with the competitive edge needed for survival and success in the marketplace of the future. These are the winners, the leaders, the ones who are the recipients of job offers time and time again! These are the candidates who cause so much excitement about their employment candidacies—the ones employers scramble to hire. And this is the employment strategy they so frequently use.

If you are to be successful in applying the five-minute strategy, you must know what questions to ask the employer, and you must practice to perfect it. The first five minutes are critical, and you must be fully prepared to make effective use of this precious time. You cannot allow yourself to be trapped into the traditional interview if you plan to emerge victorious from the interview process.

Chapter 9, "Implementing the Five-Minute Concept," is devoted to helping you get started during that first five minutes. It will teach you some practical techniques for interviewing and changing the direction of the interview during the critical first five minutes, so that you can gain an understanding of the organization's strategic goals and objectives. These techniques will provide you with the ability to collect the essential information you will need to allow you to formulate and execute hard-hitting and effective interview strategy.

9

Implementing
the Five-Minute
Concept

Becoming proficient in the use of the five-minute interview strategy requires some advance preparation and practice. It will not come simply by reading this book. You will need to learn some basic techniques, and you will need to practice them until you are confident that you can apply them in the actual interview. This practice is what I call the five-minute drill.

There are essentially three ingredients that guarantee the success of the five-minute interview strategy. The first is knowing what questions to ask. The second is knowing how to ask these questions. And, finally, the third is knowing when to ask these questions.

In this chapter, we will explore the importance of these three ingredients in the effective application of the five-minute interview strategy.

KEY QUESTIONS

As I have repeatedly said, the main focus of the five-minute interview concept is on the strategic goals and objectives of the organization. You must therefore have some understanding of where the organization is headed before you can effectively position yourself as someone who can help bring about positive change within the organization.

Here are key "five-minute" questions which I am sure will prove helpful to you in defining those changes that the organization wishes to bring about and the corresponding employment qualifications needed for good performance:

1. What are the key strategic objectives of the organization?

2. What are the key shifts or changes in direction that the organization is attempting to bring about?

3. What effect will these shifts or changes have on the department or function in which I will be working?

4. What new results will be expected of the department? Why?

5. What current responsibilities will become obsolete?

6. How will these overall changes affect the responsibilities of the position for which I am interviewing?

7. What new results will this position be responsible for? Why?

8. What current responsibilities will become obsolete?

9. What aspects of the current position will likely remain unchanged?

10. Considering these changes, what qualifications do you feel will be needed to ensure successful job performance?

11. Which of thee qualifications do you feel will be most important? Why?

12. Which will be least important? Why?

You will notice that the foregoing questions are designed to allow the candidate to define the major changes that the organization wishes to bring about at the corporate, functional, and job level. Helping the organization to bring about positive change in any of these key areas would be seen as "value adding" to the organization since these are the areas thought by the organization to be critical to business success. Thus, by citing your capability to positively impact any of these important areas, you will automatically classify yourself as a positive change agent who has the potential to bring improvement and added value to the organization.

You will also note that this list of questions is fairly extensive. Therefore, it is not practical for you to think that you will have time to ask all of these questions during the first five minutes of the interview. This being the case, it is advisable for you to select only five or six of these for use at the onset of the interview. Save the remaining questions for use later in the interview.

My suggestion is that you select those questions that are of greatest strategic importance to the organization (numbers 1, 2, 3, 4, 6, and 7). These seem to do a good job of focusing on the organization's strategic thrust as well as on those changes that the organization feels must be effected in order to realize its mission and objectives. Thoughtful answers to these questions will provide you with an excellent framework against which to operate in presenting yourself as an ideal candidate for the position.

It is important that you feel comfortable with the specific wording of these key questions. The words used above are mine. Chances are, if you attempt to memorize them, you will tend to feel unnatural and uncomfortable, and you will come across as being superficial. Worse yet, you may feel anxious and nervous, which will cause you to lose your self-confidence. In most cases, your anxiety will be evident to the interviewer and will detract from your overall presentation effectiveness.

Therefore, as a first exercise, I recommend that you select five or six key questions that you wish to ask during the first five minutes of the interview, and try rephrasing them in your own language. Use the space provided for this purpose.

1. _____

_____

_____

_____

2. _____

_____

_____

3. _____

_____

_____

4. _____

_____

_____

5. _____

_____

_____

6. _____

_____

_____

INTERVIEW TECHNIQUES

Although discussed earlier in this book, it is important, when designing your key questions, that you use effective interviewing techniques. In this way, you will assure that you will be receiving the maximum amount of relevant information on which to base your five-minute interview strategy.

Here are a few simple rules to follow that should prove helpful to you. For a more in-depth review of these, see Chapter 3, "Interview Techniques."

1. Do not ask questions that require a simple yes or no answer.

2. Start your questions with the same words that have proven so successful for journalists for years:
   What.
   Where.
   When.
   Who.
   Why.
   How.

3. To prove an area more deeply, follow an initial question with additional questions from the foregoing list.

4. Use comparison or contrast questions such as:
   How would you *compare* X to Y?
   How would you *contrast* A to B?

5. For further clarification, ask for examples.

As is often the case, *how* you go about asking a question can be as important as *what* you are asking. How you ask the question will determine the depth and quality of the answer. Simple or superficial questions will not suffice if you are to get the kind of information you will need to plan and implement a hard-hitting and effective interview strategy. You should, therefore, pay particular attention to these important techniques when designing your five-minute interview questions.

TIMING

Timing is critical to the success of the five-minute interview strategy. You will need to "get out of the box" early if you are to redirect the flow of the discussion to focus the attention of the interviewer on the critical questions that you will need answered in order to formulate your five-minute strategy. It is imperative, therefore, that these questions be addressed early in the interview discussion if you are to have sufficient time to plan an effective strategy.

If you wait too long to introduce your key questions, you will likely find yourself locked into a traditional interview structure from which it will be difficult to extract yourself without seeming rude or insensitive to your host. Thus, it is important that you "get your oar in the water," so to speak, right from the beginning. To do this, you will need to assert yourself early in the discussion. However, such assertiveness must be tempered with appropriate sensitivity.

PROPER SENSITIVITY

The important thing to remember, when planning to intervene in the interview structure, is that most interviewers need to feel that they are in control of the interview process. Although professional interviewers can usually "roll with the punches" and tolerate a certain amount of disruption of their planned line of questioning, such interruption can prove very threatening to those with less experience. Unfortunately, there are many more inexperienced interviewers than there are seasoned pros.

Simply put, the threat to the inexperienced interviewer is that there may not be sufficient time to ask all of the questions necessary

to arrive at a well-founded employment decision. Thus, any interruption of the interview plan poses the possibility that there will be
insufficient time for proper questioning of the candidate. This can
cause the interviewer to feel nervous and generally uneasy. There
is also the danger that the interviewer will be preoccupied with re-
gaining control of the interview and may, therefore, not be listening to what you are saying. When this happens, precious time can
be lost, and it may take considerable effort to reestablish the personal rapport that is so critical to favorable interview results.

The answer to this problem is simple. You will need to develop some techniques that will allow you to intervene early in the
interview discussion without threatening the interviewer with loss
of control of the interview process. I will be providing you with
some suggested techniques later in this chapter, but first we will
need to discuss the matter of interview "framing."

FRAMING THE INTERVIEW

During the introductory phase of the interview, most experienced
interviewers (following the basic greeting and small talk) will
frame the interview. The purpose of this framing is to provide the
candidate with some understanding of the areas to be discussed,
thereby helping the candidate to feel more comfortable with the
ensuing interview process. The following are two examples of
framing:

1. Mr. Jones, as you know, we will be discussing the position
   of division controller. In order to determine whether we
   have a good match here, it will be necessary to get to
   know a lot about you and your background. We will,

therefore, be exploring a number of areas. These will include your educational background, previous positions you have held, your experience, and your accomplishments. We will also wish to discuss some of the softer sides of your qualifications such as personal style, your operating style, and your overall management philosophy. In this way, we will get to know you well and be in a better position to determine whether we will have a good match here. This decision, I'm sure you'll agree, is very important to both of us. Perhaps a good place to start is with your educational background. Where did you go to school?

2. As you know, during our interview today we will be discussing the position of chief project engineer. Although we will want to cover your overall background very thoroughly, we are particularly interested in your experience as chief engineer with the Garrott Corporation. We would like to gain some insight into the scope of your position at Garrott as well as some of your major accomplishments. But first, Ms. Cameron, let's explore your educational background. What were the factors that led to your decision to major in mechanical engineering?

You will notice that in both of these introductions, the interviewer has taken the time to give the candidate some sense of where the interview will be headed. This is normally followed by some sort of introductory question that is intended to get the discussion started.

As mentioned earlier if you are to successfully implement the five-minute interview strategy, it will be necessary for you to skillfully intervene during the first couple of minutes of the interview, redirecting the flow of the discussion to focus on those critical questions that you will need to have answered. This is not an easy matter, and will require some practice on your part. You should find the following "intervention techniques" helpful in accomplishing this objective.

INTERVENTION TECHNIQUES

To implement the five-minute strategy, there are three points at which you can intervene during the introductory phase of the employment interview. These are (1) before the interview is framed, (2) after the interview is framed, and (3) after the first question has been asked by the interviewer. These are listed in order of preference.

It should be fairly obvious that by asking your key five-minute questions immediately following the introduction and small talk, but before the interviewer has had time to frame the interview discussion, there will be the least disruption of the interview plan. Although still causing some feelings of uneasiness on the part of the interviewer, there is less danger of loss of control at this stage of the interview and, therefore, the interviewer will tend to feel less threatened if interrupted. Therefore, where possible, it is strongly recommended that you intervene in the interview discussion.

Once the interview has been framed, however, it is far more difficult to comfortably intervene. By that point, the interviewer has already set forth the basic interview plan, and your intrusion is far more evident. Interruption at this stage is seen by the interviewer as more confrontational and a possible threat to his or her control. Therefore, you will need to handle this intervention with far greater sensitivity if you wish to minimize this threat and still maintain a reasonable amount of personal rapport with your host.

Finally, once the interviewer has framed the interview discussion, and followed this with a direct question, it becomes exceedingly difficult to intervene in the process without posing a serious and very noticeable threat to the interviewer. In such cases it becomes painfully clear to the interviewer that you have your own agenda and are willing to directly challenge for control of the interview process. Intervention at this point, therefore, calls for extreme sensitivity and tactful language on your part.

The techniques illustrated in the following examples are provided to assist you in intervening at various stages during the introductory phases of the interview process. They are carefully worded so as to convey proper respect for the interviewer's position and to recognize the need for the interviewer to maintain control of the interview. You will also note that these statements are worded in such a way as to be sure that absolute control remains with the interviewer.

BEFORE THE INTERVIEW IS FRAMED

Before we get started, Ms. Jones, *I would appreciate* it if you could answer a few important questions for me.

Ms. Jones, since we have limited time and I know you will need to focus on those areas of my background that are important, *I'm wondering if you would mind* answering some key questions for me.

Ms. Jones, in order that we may maximize our time together, and focus on those items that will be most important to you, *I'm wondering if you would mind* answering a few preliminary questions about the company and the position before we get started with the formal interview.

Perhaps, before we get started, Ms. Jones, you could provide me with some general information about the job and the company. *I would appreciate* it if you could answer a few important questions for me.

Before we get started, Ms. Jones, there are a couple of things that *I would like* to know about the position and the company. It *would be helpful* to have some answers to a few basic questions so that I am sure to focus on those aspects of my background that will be of greatest interest to you.

AFTER THE INTERVIEW IS FRAMED

This certainly sounds like a logical approach to our interview. However, *I was wondering if you might* take a few moments before we get started to answer some key questions I have. I feel this could help us to have a very meaningful discussion.

Sounds like a thorough approach to me. However, before we get started *I would appreciate it if you could* answer a few important questions for me.

This sounds like a good approach. However, before we get started, Ms. Jones, *I would appreciate it if you wouldn't mind* answering a few brief questions. This will help me to have a fuller appreciation of where we are headed and what kind of things will be of particular interest to you.

Ms. Jones, *I appreciate* your sharing your interview approach with me. However, it would be helpful, before we get started, *if you* could answer a few key questions for me. *Would you mind?*

Ms. Jones, that sounds like a good approach to me. However, before we get started, *I would appreciate it if you could* answer a few important questions for me. This will help me to focus on those items that are of most importance to you.

AFTER THE FIRST QUESTION HAS BEEN ASKED

Ms. Jones, I'd be pleased to answer your question, but, before we get involved in discussing the details of my background, *I would appreciate it if you could* take a little time to answer a few general questions for me. This would help me to have a better understanding of where we are headed. *Do you mind?*

Ms. Jones, I'd be pleased to answer your question, but before I do, *if you wouldn't mind,* I'd like to ask a few basic questions about the position. This will help me to focus better on those aspects of my background that are of greatest importance to your decision process. *Would you mind?*

Ms. Jones, I realize that this is an important question, but before we get started, *I would appreciate it if you could* answer a few basic questions concerning the position. *Do you mind?*

Ms. Jones, your interest in my educational background is important. However, before we get too far along in our interview, *would you mind* clarifying a few key items for me?

I'm glad you asked that question since my education appears well-suited to your needs. However, before we get started with my educational background, *I was wondering if you could* first answer a few general questions for me.

A good question, Ms. Jones, but before we begin a detailed discussion of my background, *I was wondering if you could* help me understand a few general points concerning the job requirements. *Would you mind?*

I'd be happy to answer your question, Ms. Jones, but, *if you will excuse my interruption,* there are a few general questions that I would like to pursue before we get off into the details of my background. *Do you mind?*

You will notice that throughout the preceding examples of intervention techniques I have italicized key words and phrases. These words and phrases play an important role in the effectiveness of these techniques. They show deference toward the interviewer and tend to reduce the threat that can be posed by loss of interview control.

Phrases like "would you mind," "I would appreciate if you could," "perhaps you could," "it would be helpful if you could," and so on suggest that the interviewer clearly has some options. These phrases tend to show respect for the interviewer's right to control the discussion while substantially reducing the threat, and resultant anxiety, posed by the potential loss of control of the interview. Use of these, or similar words, will be critical to your ability to successfully intervene and carry out your five-minute interview strategy.

Successful execution of the five-minute concept will require that you become proficient in the use of these intervention techniques. Therefore it is imperative that you practice these techniques until you are thoroughly familiar and comfortable with them. Be particularly careful with the wording so that you reduce the degree of threat to the interviewer. As with the key interview questions discussed earlier in this chapter, it is important that these techniques be adapted by you so that you will feel more at home and comfortable with the wording. This will relax you and enhance your interviewing effectiveness.

FIVE-MINUTE DRILL

You are now ready for the five-minute drill. To carry this drill out successfully, you will need to do two things:

1. Choose the intervention technique(s) with which you feel most comfortable.
2. Choose five or six key actual interview questions that you wish to use during the five-minute drill.

Now, find a partner with whom you will feel comfortable, and have this partner play the role of the interviewer. Using the following script, have your partner read the basic interview introduction as written. Practice interrupting at different points during the introductory remarks, using the various intervention techniques that you have just learned in this chapter. Follow these by introducing your key interview questions. Have your partner ad lib the answers to these questions so that you get accustomed to their variety. Continue this process repeatedly until you are thoroughly comfortable with your ability to make a smooth transition regardless of the circumstances with which you are confronted.

INTERVIEW SCRIPT ONE

Interviewer: Good morning Jim, I'm pleased you could join us today. How was your trip?

Candidate: (Response)

Interviewer: Well, I'm pleased you were able to join us and am looking forward to our discussion here this morning.

(Pause)

> As you know, Jim, we will be talking to you about a position here at Baker as (<u>name of position</u>). This is an important position to us, and it is important that we have just the right person to fill it. I'm sure you feel that it is equally important that this position be a good fit for you as well. Therefore, it is important that we use our time effectively to gain a thorough understanding of your qualifications. This way we will be in a better position to determine if we have a good two-way fit. It is important to both of us that we thoroughly explore your background so that we get to know you well. I want to explore your early childhood, your educational background, and your work experience. I would also like to discuss your major accomplishments, your personal style, your operating style, and your overall management philosophy.

(Pause)

> Perhaps we could start with your early childhood. Jim, where did you grow up?

Candidate: (Use intervention technique followed by key questions.)

INTERVIEW SCRIPT TWO

Interviewer: Good morning, Jim. Nice day we're having out there!

Candidate: (Response)

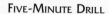

Interviewer: What did you think of the president's speech on television last night? Did you hear it?

Candidate: (Response)

Interviewer: Well, enough of politics. Perhaps we should get down to the business at hand.

Candidate: (Use intervention technique followed by key interview questions.)

ADDITIONAL PRACTICE

It will be necessary for you to go through several mock interviews with your interview partner in order for you to become thoroughly proficient in the use of the five-minute interview strategy. To accomplish this, and to enable you to experience as much variety as possible, try your hand at designing your own interview scripts. As with any activity that requires skill, the more you practice, the more effective you will become at executing the five-minute interview strategy.

10

The "Voids" Strategy

An interview strategy that is very similar to the five-minute interview is the "voids" strategy. The focus of the five-minute strategy, as previously discussed, is on the strategic direction and goals of the hiring organization. By contrast, the focus of the voids strategy is on the existing position. The emphasis of this strategy is on discovering opportunities for performance improvement (the voids) in the current position, with the employment candidate then positioning him or herself as someone who can add value to the organization by filling these voids.

Essentially, performance voids are of two types. The first of these are what I call "nonperformance" items. These are aspects of the position that currently are not performed at all. The second are what I call "poor performance" items—those key aspects of the position that, although currently carried out, are being performed at a substandard level.

In the eyes of the employer, both nonperformance and poor performance items represent opportunities to bring about improvement and add value to the organization. As with the five-minute interview approach, the voids strategy allows the candidate to position himself or herself as a positive change agent who can add value to the organization.

I have seen the voids strategy used very effectively as interviewing strategy over the years. Historically speaking, it has proven equally as effective as the five-minute interview strategy and, where effectively employed, has accounted for many job offers. However, due to the enormous competitive pressures now being placed on most organizations and the resulting emphasis on competitive strategy, the five-minute strategy, with its focus on helping the organization to achieve its strategic goals, will prove to be the stronger of these two important approaches.

Nevertheless, the voids strategy is one that should definitely be part of your arsenal of employment interview weapons. It can prove to be an extremely effective technique in creating interest in your employment candidacy and in generating employment offers. I strongly suggest that you not overlook it.

DEFINING PERFORMANCE VOIDS

The key to designing an effective voids interview strategy is to define those performance areas of the existing position that the employer feels could be improved. As with the five-minute strategy, this must be done sufficiently early in the interview to allow you the time to formulate an effective, hard-hitting strategy that will address these major opportunity areas.

Here are some key questions that you can employ during the interview discussion to define these performance voids:

1. In your opinion, what aspects of the current position could be better performed?

2. In what ways could performance be improved?

3. Which of these performance improvement areas is most important to the organization?

4. Why is improvement in these areas important?

5. Are there any key responsibilities or objectives of this position which are not currently being met at all? What are they?

6. Which of these do you consider important? Why?

7. What factors have prevented accomplishment of these important responsibilities/objectives?

8. In general, what overall improvements would you like to see in this position?

9. Which of these do you consider most important?

10. What would you most like to see a new employee in this position do to bring about improvement to the function?

Answers to these questions will provide you with a host of performance opportunity areas on which you can focus in designing an effective interview strategy that will capture the employer's attention. Positioning yourself as a positive change agent in any of these important opportunity areas should certainly create some real interest in your employment candidacy.

PAST INCUMBENTS

Many times the hiring manager will tailor the candidate specification to the profiles of people who have previously been in the position. This can work in both directions.

If the past incumbent was considered to be highly successful, the employer's thought process is one that says, "What I need is someone like good old Joe. Joe really performed exceptionally well in this job. Now, let's see, what was Joe's educational background and prior experience when he entered this position? What was there about Joe and his operating style that made him particularly effective?" This tendency to tailor the candidate specification after a particularly successful past incumbent is what I call the "halo" profile.

In contrast with the halo profile is the "loser" profile. As I'm sure you have guessed, this is the profile represented by past incumbents whose performance was considered to be less than satisfactory.

There is something to be learned from poor performers as well, since most employers would not like to duplicate their experience by hiring someone who has essentially the same profile and qualifications as these poor performers. When constructing the loser profile, the hiring manager will go through a very similar thought process: "John was really a problem in this job. What I really don't need is another John in this position! Let's see, what was John's education and experience when he was hired? What education and/or experience did he lack that Joe had? How about his operating style? What aspects of John's style did not fit in well with our operating environment?"

The process described here is not untypical of what many hiring managers go through when defining candidate selection criteria. For many employers, this examination of past incumbents' performance, and contrast between successful performers and poor performers, has proven an effective method for arriving at these criteria over the years. If used carefully, it can provide some meaningful insight.

When planning an interview strategy as an interviewee, it can be very helpful to force yourself to think like the employer. Thus, you must ask a lot of the same questions that the employer does. Duplicating the same logic employed by the hiring manager in defining the candidate specification is what I call the "mirror" strategy. This approach can be very revealing as to the type of person the employer is seeking and can provide a significant competitive advantage in the interview process.

Obviously, you don't have the opportunity to observe past incumbents in the position, but you do have the opportunity to ask questions about them of the employer. However, this must be done with discretion and you must avoid asking sensitive questions that will put the interviewer on the spot.

Usually the interviewer will be willing to discuss the profile and performance of good performers in some detail. However, this is not the case with poor performers, so you will need to tread lightly when asking questions in this area. Generally, the way to avoid this possible sensitivity is to talk about poor performers as a category rather than to discuss specific individuals who fit into it.

The following are questions you can use to probe these important areas and secure the kind of information that should help formulate an effective interview strategy:

1. Of the past incumbents who have held this position, what has been characteristic of the better performers?

2. What kinds of things did they do particularly well?

3. Why were these things important?

4. What qualifications did they possess that made them particularly effective in this position?

5. Was there something unique about their knowledge, skills, or operating style? What?

6. Has there been anyone whose performance has really stood out from the rest?

7. What was unique about this individual that made him or her so outstanding?

8. What did this person do that others have not?

9. Of the past incumbents who have held this position, what has been characteristic of those who have performed poorly?

10. What aspects of the position were usually performed poorly?

11. In what ways did their performance fall short?

12. What impact did this have?

13. How could their performance have been improved?

14. Was there anything that these individuals uniformly lacked that contributed to this poor performance (i.e., knowledge, skills, experience, style)?

15. How did these deficiencies reflect in their performance?

Having asked these questions, you are now in a unique position. First and foremost, you have forced the employer to think more deeply about those qualifications felt to be most important to good job performance. Second, you now know what qualifications are important to the employer, almost from the beginning of the interview. Your strategy now becomes one of comparing yourself to past winners and contrasting yourself with past losers.

EMPHASIZE THE POSITIVE

As you review the answers provided to you by the employer about those who have performed particularly well in the position, you are able to determine two things: you are able to determine what aspects of the position the employer considers important areas to perform well in, and you are also able to determine the qualifications the employer considers important to good performance. Thus, you have an opportunity to emphasize the positive aspects of both your qualifications and past performance in such a way as to frame yourself as the ideal candidate for the position.

To do this effectively, you will need to ask yourself the following questions early in the interview:

1. What were the important aspects of the job in which good performers tended to perform well?
2. What evidence can I give of my own good performance in similar job areas?
3. What key qualifications did the employer feel were essential to good performance?
4. Which of these qualifications do I possess?
5. What evidence can I give of my qualifications in these areas?

FILL THE VOIDS

Also, as you review the answers provided to you by the employer about past job incumbents who have performed poorly, be on the lookout for performance or qualifications voids that you can fill. To fill these voids, you will need to provide specific evidence of qualifications and/or experience that you have that will serve to fill the performance gaps left by these poor performers.

In order to effectively do this, you will need to ask yourself the following questions during the interview:

1. What aspects of the position did poor performers tend to perform particularly poorly in?
2. What evidence can I give of good performance in these or similar areas?

3. What qualifications did these poor performers appear to lack?

4. In which of these qualification areas am I particularly strong?

Having defined your strengths in these key performance and qualifications areas, you are in a position to contrast your capabilities with those who have performed poorly, showing that these are areas of particular strength for you. Thus, you are able to fill these past performance voids rather nicely and can frame yourself in a way that the employer will see as value adding—someone who will perform well in these critical areas and who will bring about improvement to the organization.

11

The "Ideal Candidate" Strategy

If you are determined to win in the interview game and come away with an employment offer, there is another interview strategy that you can employ to gain a competitive edge in the interview process. This is known as the "ideal candidate" strategy.

Although not always well-defined in advance of the interview, employers usually do have a general vision of the "ideal candidate" in mind, which is used as the benchmark for evaluating employment candidates. One way of gaining a significant competitive advantage in the interview is to attempt to get the employer to share this "ideal profile" with you, so that you have a better understanding of the criteria the employer considers important in the selection of a finalist candidate for the position.

To gain maximum mileage from use of this strategy, apply this approach early in the interview discussion—preferably, within the first five to ten minutes of the interview. In this way, you will have a clear understanding of those qualifications the employer considers most important to candidate selection right from the onset, allowing sufficient time for you to focus on (and emphasize) your qualifications that best align with the employer's ideal vision.

AVOID BEING TOO OBVIOUS

When employing the ideal candidate strategy, avoid being too obvious in your approach. Direct attempts to have the employer describe the "ideal candidate" will often cause seasoned interviewers to be evasive and to attempt to defer their answer until later in the interview (after they have had a chance to evaluate your qualifications). Don't ask direct questions such as, "How would you describe the ideal candidate for this position?" This is far too obvious.

Trained interviewers are exceptionally cautious about tipping their hand concerning the candidate qualifications they are seeking. They do not wish to unduly influence the outcome of the interview by allowing you the opportunity to adjust your answers to interview questions to fit a predetermined profile. Instead, they much prefer to "keep you in the dark," preferring you to be as spontaneous as possible in answering their interview questions. By not influencing you, they feel that they will get a far more accurate reading of your qualifications for the job.

If you were to use a direct approach and ask a skilled interviewer to describe the ideal candidate for the position, you are likely to get a response similar to the following. "Joan, that's a good question. Although I'm certainly willing to give you an answer, I would prefer to defer my answer until later in our discussion. I do not wish to influence your answers to my interview questions, and feel I need to first get to know more about you. Why don't we proceed with the interview, and I will return to your question a little later in our discussion." If you are going to employ the ideal candidate strategy, your approach needs to be far more subtle.

A CONTRARY VIEW

As the employment candidate, it is clearly not to your advantage to be "kept in the dark" if you are going to optimize your chances for success in the interview. To improve your chances of getting a job offer, it is important for you to understand what the employer considers to be the most important candidate selection attributes. Having this insight, particularly early in the interview process, will allow you to focus on those qualifications that will cast you in the most favorable light, and motivate the employer to hire you. From your perspective, it is important to pry this information from the interviewer, if at all possible.

Before moving on to some strategies for making this happen, a mild word of caution is in order. Unless you are desperate for a job, it is not advisable to "force fit" yourself into a job for which you are not qualified, or which will prove to be dissatisfying. So, although you may wish to be somewhat "commercial" in your answers to interview questions (i.e., slanting answers to fit the employer's ideal candidate profile), you should avoid overselling or misrepresenting your qualifications for a job that is clearly not a good fit for you. Life is too short to intentionally place yourself in a position for which you are ill-qualified or where it is clear from the start that you will be unhappy.

THE INDIRECT APPROACH

Rather than directly asking the employer to describe the "ideal candidate" for this position, you will want to take a less obvious tact when employing the "ideal candidate" strategy. Here are some different ways to ask the same question, where your intended strategy will not be quite so obvious to the employer.

1. As you think about the challenges of this position, what do you feel is most important for success?

2. What do you feel is required for success in this job?

3. What do you feel are the most important competencies required for success in this position, and why do you feel these are important?

4. When reviewing the performance of past incumbents in this position, what appear to be the attributes that have consistently accounted for success?

5. In your opinion, what does it take to be highly successful in this job?

As you can see, these questions are a far more subtle way of applying the "ideal candidate strategy." Using this indirect approach, however, is far more likely to get you the information you need than if you used the direct approach (i.e., asking the employer to describe the ideal candidate). Yet, the answers you get to these questions are likely to come very close to describing the ideal profile sought by the employer.

As emphasized earlier, it is important that you apply this strategy as early as possible in the interview. This will provide you with the insight needed to focus on those areas of your qualifications most likely to be of greatest interest to the employer. The competitive advantage of employing such a strategy is obvious, and you are likely to benefit significantly from its effective use.

12

The "Key-Problems-and-Challenges" Strategy

When your objective is to significantly improve your competitive advantage in the interview and enhance your chances of success, another important approach to consider is the key-problems-and-challenges strategy. This has proven, time and again, to be a very powerful tool for turning the employment interview in the candidate's favor.

BEHIND THE STRATEGY

Behind the key-problems-and-challenges strategy is a very basic, fundamental principle that is at the very heart of the employment process. Simply stated, this principle is:

> The reason why jobs exist is the need to have someone to handle the key problems and challenges faced by the organization.

Stated differently:

> Jobs exist simply because problems and challenges exist.

If the organization did not have to solve specific problems or meet certain challenges, there would not be a need to have jobs (or people for that matter). As basic as this principle sounds, this simplistic view offers some great insight into what is important to success in the employment interview.

FROM THE EMPLOYER'S VIEWPOINT

In order to effectively use this strategy, it is important to gain some insight concerning what problems and challenges the employer sees as important to successful performance of the job. Stated differently, "What are the priorities of the job? What does the employer feel are the key problems that need to be solved and the key challenges that need to be met?" Your ability to successfully address these key concerns is going to be very important to interview success (or failure).

APPLYING THE STRATEGY

In order to create a strong interest in your employment candidacy, it is imperative that you get a clear understanding of what is important to the hiring manager as early a possible in the interview. What are the key problems and challenges facing the hiring manager—the areas that most need to be addressed in order to ensure job success? Defining these areas and gaining some idea of their relative importance during the early phase of the interview discussion can put you in a strong position to positively influence the outcome of the interview and enhance the probability of an employment offer.

Here are some key questions that you can use to gain such a competitive interview advantage:

1. What do you feel are some of the key challenges of this position?

2. What are some of the important problems that need to be addressed in this position?

   a. Why are these important?

   b. What are your hopes and expectations with respect to these areas?

3. What do you consider to be some of the most important challenges to be faced in this position?

4. What key problems would you most like to see tackled early in this job? Why do you consider these important priorities?

5. What do you consider to be the most pressing priorities of this position? Why?

These, and similar questions, should shed considerable insight on those elements of the job that are most important to the hiring manager. Your success in convincing the employer of your ability to address key areas of concern should go a long way to generating a considerable amount of interest in your employment candidacy.

Start, then, early in the interview to gain an understanding of the key problems and challenges you will face in the job. Understand which of these the employer considers most important, and what kind of results the employer would most like to see in these critical areas. Your effectiveness in persuading the hiring manager of your ability to make significant contributions in these important areas is bound to have a major impact on interview results and be a key factor in landing the employment offer.

Use of the key-problems-and-challenges strategy as an interview tool can put you at a distinct competitive advantage over other employment candidates, and substantially enhance the probability of interview success. It is an employment interview strategy that, if effectively employed, will prove to generate considerable interest in your employment candidacy!

13

Avoiding
Interview Disaster

Much has been written in interview books on the topic of how to succeed in the job interview, but seldom do you find much written on the topic of how to avoid interview disasters. Yet, by design, the typical employment interview is replete with opportunities for failure. How to avoid such potential failure is the focal point of this chapter.

When viewed from the employer's perspective, at the macro-level, the employment interview is structured to accomplish two fundamental objectives:

1. Screen out unqualified (or least qualified) candidates.
2. Screen in and hire the best qualified candidate.

The employment interview is every bit as much a "screening out" process as it is a "screening in" process. Much of a candidate's employment interview preparation focuses on developing the ability to describe strengths, capabilities, and accomplishments—the attributes that will help them to "make the sale." Little is normally done, however, to prepare for the other side of the equation—the factors that the employer will use to screen the candidate out.

To view this a little differently, consider the following. The employment interview is usually "won" on the positive side of the equation. This is where the candidate is able to clearly and persuasively describe his or her strengths and overall capabilities to perform the job. This is the area of the interview where candidates tend to feel most comfortable and are apt to perform at their best. On the other hand, where most interviews tend to begin to unravel and can eventually come apart, is on the opposite (the negative) side of the interview equation. It is here where the candidate is asked to describe "weaknesses," "areas for improvement," "development needs," and the like. Most job candidates feel uncomfortable sharing such negative information about themselves and, therefore, don't tend to do a very good job of it. It is precisely here, however, where most employment interviews are "lost"!

Preparing to "win" in the job interview requires solid preparation on both sides of the employment equation. You need to be prepared to effectively describe your positive attributes for the position in question. However, you also need to be equally adept, comfortable, and persuasive in fielding those tough interview questions that tend to focus on your "deficits." This chapter provides some basic principles and techniques that will help you to effectively handle those tough interview questions and thereby avoid potential interview disaster.

TOUGH INTERVIEW QUESTIONS

As already mentioned, the interview questions most difficult for the average candidate to handle are those that are intended to probe weaknesses or areas requiring the individual's improvement and/or development. The following are some examples of questions which fall into this category:

1. What are your major weaknesses?

2. In what areas could you most improve?

3. During a reference check, what would your boss likely cite as key areas for your development and performance improvement?

4. Over time, what have historically been described as the areas in which you could most improve your overall performance and effectiveness?

5. In your last performance evaluation, what areas were cited as areas in which you could improve your overall performance?

6. If we were to talk with some of your coworkers during a reference check, what areas of your performance are they likely to cite as needing improvement?

7. In what areas of your current job are you least effective?

8. If asked to be somewhat critical, what would your boss (and/or peers) cite as the two or three areas in which you could most improve?

9. With what aspects of your current position are you least comfortable? Why?

10. What aspects of your current job could be better performed? Why, and what are you doing to improve in these areas?

Unless properly fielded, each of the above interview questions is an interview disaster just waiting to happen. Regardless of how well you may have done describing your strengths and positive attributes for the job up to this point in time, nothing can send an otherwise positive interview into a fatal tailspin faster than poor answers to the above (or similar) questions. Learning how to effectively answer these questions can often spell the difference between total victory and absolute failure in the interview process.

KEY PRINCIPLES FOR HANDLING NEGATIVE INFORMATION

There are two important principles to be followed when sharing potentially "negative" information about yourself in the employment interview. These are:

1. Never make an "absolute" negative statement about yourself.
2. Always hang a "positive anchor" on any negative statement made.

To illustrate the effectiveness of these principles, consider the following two very different answers to the same self-improvement interview question:

Interview Question

> If asked to describe your operating style, how would your boss describe you? Specifically, what would he or she say would be the area most needing improvement?

Answer 1 (Absolute Negative Statement)

> I have a tendency to be overly-detailed.

Answer 2 (Applying Key Principles)

> I think she might say that, at times, I could be a little less detailed. If pressed, however, I think she would also tell you that she values my thoroughness, accuracy, and dependability.

Answer 1 illustrates a case where the candidate has made an "absolute" negative statement about him or herself. The interviewer will come away from this interview with very little doubt in his or her mind—the candidate is unquestionably "overly-detailed."

By contrast, notice, in Answer 2, how use of such carefully selected words as "might" and "at times" begins to soften the negative blow of the statement (taking it out of the realm of the "absolute," and shedding some doubt on the severity of the problem). The potential negative impact of this statement is then further diminished (if not completely neutralized) through the application of a "positive anchor" statement. The statement that "I think she would also tell you that she values my thoroughness, accuracy, and dependability" serves to greatly reduce the potential negative impact that the candidate's response might otherwise have had on interview results. It leaves a far more favorable impression on the interviewer than would otherwise have been the case!

Hopefully, this example will serve to illustrate just how effective these damage control principles can be in sharing negative information about yourself with the employer during the course of the employment interview. Now that you have seen how these principles can be applied, try applying them to the other tough interview questions previously listed in this chapter. Practice in fielding these questions and applying the basic principles just learned should serve to make you far more comfortable and effective in handling difficult questions of this type. It should also provide you with the necessary skills and confidence to artfully avoid what could otherwise prove to be some of the most dangerous pitfalls of the employment interview process.

SHIFTING THE PERCEPTION PARADIGM

When preparing to answer questions relating to weaknesses, areas for improvement, development needs, and so on, it is important to remember that "beauty is in the eye of the beholder." In this case, "perception is in the eye of the perceiver." What one perceives to be a "strength," others might see as a "weakness." Further, what some perceive to be a "weakness," others might see as a "positive attribute." It's all in the eye of the beholder.

To further illustrate this concept, consider the following illustration. In a small, entrepreneurial, start-up business, some of the attributes considered to be strengths might include:

1. Being a risk-taker.
2. The ability to make fast decisions in the absence of detailed analysis.
3. The ability to deal with ambiguity.
4. Enjoying lack of structure, variety, and fast-paced change.

By contrast, a different work environment (such as a mature, well-established business) may well value totally opposite candidate characteristics. These could include:

1. Being cautious, careful.
2. The ability to do careful, painstaking analysis as a prelude to decision making.
3. Working best in a well-defined, formal environment.
4. Liking to work in a structured, orderly, planful work environment.

Thus, the requirements of particular work environments can influence the preference for very diverse employee behaviors. It all depends upon what the specific work environment requires for performance success. There are no "absolute" standards or selection criteria that apply to all organizations universally.

Thus, in our prior example, being overly-detailed may be seen as a negative attribute in one work culture. In another, however, being very detailed could well be seen as a positive attribute. This is especially true if the organization values thoroughness, accuracy, and dependability. What one person sees as your weakness, others may well see as your strength. Take advantage of this diversity of viewpoint when preparing for the interview. The positive anchor approach, as previously described and illustrated, can be used to effectively shift the paradigm from negative to positive if intelligently employed in the interview.

When practicing the answers to the tough questions listed earlier in this chapter, try playing shift the paradigm. First list your potential negative attributes, and then restate these same attributes in such a way that they can be perceived as strengths. See how creative you can get. For example:

Negative Attribute	Strength
Overly detailed	Thorough, accurate
Serious, intense	Dedicated, committed
Demanding	Efficient, productive
Slow	Careful, accurate, quality-conscious
Impatient	Productive, fast-paced
Insensitive	Results-focused

After identifying your negatives and their corresponding positive attributes, a good way to practice handling these tough questions

(and get comfortable with them) is to apply the following basic formula.

> Some people might describe me as (*negative attribute*), but others would tell you that I am (*positive attribute*).

or

> Some people might say that I have a tendency to (*negative attribute*) but others, who know me well, would tell you that I am (*positive attribute*).

This approach can go a long way toward helping you to comfortably talk about potential shortcomings with an employer, without totally destroying your employment chances in the process. If practiced, and used effectively, it is a strategy that can prove most effective in neutralizing the potentially negative effect that "self-criticism" could otherwise have on the success of the interview process.

TIPS FOR HANDLING NEGATIVE INFORMATION

Tips for handling potentially negative information about yourself in the interview discussion include the following:

1. Thoroughly prepare for tough interview questions *before* the interview.

2. Emphasize the positives, de-emphasize the negatives.

3. Be "short, sweet, and to-the-point"—then quickly transition to your strengths and positives.

4. Don't be embarrassed or overly-apologetic about your shortcomings. Everybody has them! Be confident and matter-of-fact.

5. Don't volunteer your "worst" negatives; choose those shortcomings that are "least damaging" (especially ones where you have shown some improvement).

6. Neutralize the impact of negative information you share by:

   a. Stating that the negative has not been a "major" issue (i.e., it has not interfered with your overall performance).

   b. Citing how some would perceive this negative trait differently. (Some might see it as a strength.)

   c. Putting it in a "historical context" (i.e., past bosses never saw this as a problem—offer these bosses as references to verify this).

Following these tips should help you effectively exercise good damage control in the interview and avoid the traps that can so often lead to interview disasters and loss of good career/employment opportunities.

14

Organizational
Compatibility

As you consider the various employment opportunities that may be available to you, one area you should pay considerable attention to is "organizational compatibility." Organizational compatibility means how well you will fit into the organizational environment of the prospective employer. This chapter is intended to help you measure this important aspect of your employment decision.

Probably, of all the selection criteria used in measuring the potential for a successful employment marriage, organizational compatibility is the least understood and, as a result, the most commonly ignored. This is true of both the employer and prospective employee during the interview process. With few exceptions, the extent of attempting to measure this important element by most employers is to ask themselves, "How did I like the candidate?" The typical response is, "I thought he was a nice person," or, "I didn't think she would fit in very well. She seems somewhat aggressive."

This appears as a somewhat shallow approach, considering the importance of this selection criterion to the probability of a happy, productive, and enduring relationship. Perhaps there is something more that could be done to improve the selection process to achieve more meaningful results in this area. I certainly think so!

It has often fascinated me that one of the selling ploys, frequently used by executive search firms when selling their professional wares, is the ability of the firm to understand organizational climate and to, therefore, somehow magically pick the "right" person for the client company. Having been interviewed by several such firms, I'm often not convinced that the consultant made much of an attempt to accomplish this. Fortunately, however, there have been a few who have done a reasonable job, and have convinced me that there are still a few quality, professional firms out there.

Up to this point, I have been talking as if the responsibility for measuring organizational compatibility rests solely with the hiring organization, or its agent. Actually, I believe this couldn't be further from the truth. This is a shared responsibility, and it rests with both the candidate and the hiring organization. After all, both have an awful lot to lose if things don't work out. On your side of the ledger, for example, there is a record of failure that could jeopardize future employment and career advancement (both critical items in their own right), loss of income, social embarrassment, depletion of financial assets (savings, investments, real estate, etc.), let alone the mental anguish, depression, and loss of self-esteem that often accompany job failure. This can be devastating. It can also be avoided with a careful, well-planned interviewing strategy designed to measure this compatibility. This chapter will help you to develop such a strategy. But, first let me share a short story with you that will help convey the importance of organizational compatibility in an even more meaningful way.

John Daren (not his real name) was a highly qualified financial executive with excellent educational and experience credentials. He graduated from the Wharton School of the University of Pennsylvania with an MBA concentration in finance. Following a short stint with a Philadelphia bank as a financial analyst, John went to work for a prominent area manufacturer as an assistant controller, reporting to the division controller of a small manufacturing division. Daren was an intelligent, conscientious, and hard-working employee, and it wasn't long before top management took stock of his capability and moved him upstairs to the position of director of corporate accounting, reporting directly to the vice president and corporate controller. Although this was an extraordinary promotion with considerable added managerial responsibility, John continued to prove his mettle by working hard and turning in what the controller considered to be outstanding performance. He was awarded in kind with good salary increases and better-than-average incentive bonuses.

The company Daren worked for was considered to be a somewhat conservative, staid organization that was in a fairly mature market. Although it succeeded in maintaining market share in its important product brands, there was little innovation and the organization had reached a comfortable level of profitability with little desire or need for change. Managerial focus seemed directed more toward installing systems and improving the efficiency of existing operations than on building new business. Hence, it was in what one might refer to as a "maintenance" mode.

Although John worked diligently for a few years and continued to receive more than ample financial reward for his contributions, it wasn't very long before he began to get concerned about his prospects for future advancement. His immediate boss was only 46 years old and the corporate vice president of administrative services, to whom his boss reported, only 52. This, coupled with the firm's lack of aggressive growth plans, suggested to John that he might have to remain in the same place for several years, an unpleasant thought for someone still early in a professional career. Consequently, John made the decision to quietly look around.

Daren's search led him to a small, but rapidly growing, high tech firm, where he interviewed for the position of vice president of finance. This position reported to the president and had full responsibility for firm's financial and accounting functions. Annual growth had averaged about 25 percent over the past five years and profits were equally impressive. What made this a particularly attractive situation was the fact that the company was planning three new businesses over the next two years, and John was led to believe that he might well be a candidate to head up one of these operations as president. When he was eventually offered the position of vice president of finance at a salary of $100,000 (a 26 percent improvement over prior earnings), John was quick to accept and to move on to his new assignment. The future looked considerably brighter than before!

During the first two months, John went through the normal adjustment period that anyone encounters when making a major change in career direction. Although reasonably comfortable with the technical nature of the accounting and financial systems, he sensed there was something missing in his personal relationships with other top management personnel. At first, he passed this off as part of the transition process, rationalizing that it would simply take time for his new colleagues to adjust to the differences in operating style between himself and his predecessor. After all, he was better educated and had a more sophisticated understanding of financial and accounting matters, something that his new management would come to appreciate as a valuable addition. It soon became evident that this was not the case.

Approximately six months into the job, John Daren was asked to step into the president's office.

"John," the president started out, "it appears that things are not going to work out, and I'm going to have to call for your resignation." Shocked, Daren sat back in his chair and momentarily stared up at the ceiling. "Why?" he managed in a somewhat shaky voice. "Well," said the president, "it seems that you're not fitting in with the rest of the management team. You're used to a much more rigid environment than what we have here.

"As you know, we're relatively young and somewhat un-structured. We pride ourselves in being entrepreneurial risk takers. The nature of our business requires this. The time demands on our management team are very great, and we need people who can quickly weigh the facts, make a decision, and get on with it. We don't have time for a lot of sophisticated, time-consuming analysis. It seems to me that your analytical skills could be better used in a different kind of organization than ours.

"I'm sorry that things haven't worked out, and I regret having to take this action, but in the long run I'm sure that you're going to be much happier as a result of this decision. Donald Jones, our human resources manager, is prepared to discuss your termination benefits. He is in the next office and is prepared to talk with you right away. Again, John, I'm sorry that things couldn't have worked out differently."

Sound familiar? This is a scenario that is played out time and time again, several times a day throughout the offices of corporate America. What have we learned from this dreaded confrontation that can serve us well in the interview process? This is a question well worth pondering and, if possible, acting on.

Yes, the incompatibility issue is something that needs to be dealt with in the employment process. Put in more positive terms, organizational compatibility needs to be given more than just lip service as an employment selection criterion. Ways need to be found to more effectively gauge the probability of organizational fit during the interview process, and lessen (if not eliminate) the danger of costly and unpleasant terminations.

Aside from the pain and anguish suffered by the unfortu-nate employee, terminations are also very costly to the termi-nating organization. In addition to the emotional toll and stress that it causes for the management personnel involved in the termination process, there are also some very real financial costs to the terminating organization as well. These costs are both direct and indirect.

Direct costs are considered to be those costs that are a direct result of the termination process itself. First, there is the cost of severance pay and benefits, usually amounting to several thousand dollars. In the case of senior executives, such costs can be very significant. Second, there is the increased cost of unemployment compensation resulting from an unfavorable experience rate (the more terminations an employer has, the greater the percentage the employer has to pay to the state's unemployment insurance fund). Dependent on company policy, there may also be the cost of professional outplacement services provided to the displaced employee. Again, these services can cost several thousands of dollars, depending on the employee's hierarchical level and the extent of the services provided. Although always discussed in the most hushed of tones, there is also the potential liability suit for wrongful discharge and resulting damage to the firm's professional reputation. This has the potential to make all other costs pale by comparison.

Although few companies ever stop to consider the indirect costs of a termination, these are very real and can often exceed the direct costs. Since these costs are harder to identify, very few organizations take the time to give them much thought. Let's take a few moments to have a look at these important cost factors.

First let's consider direct replacement costs—those costs directly incurred in replacing the employee with a qualified candidate. Depending on job level and complexity of the position to be filled, replacement may well require the service of an executive search consulting firm or an employment agency. Also, it will likely involve running a recruitment ad in a newspaper or trade journal.

Both advertising costs and employment consulting fees can run in the thousands of dollars.

Perhaps the most significant indirect cost is lost productivity. Since the terminated employee was a poor fit to begin with, chances are he or she was not very productive. Finally, there is the loss of efficiency and productivity resulting from the learning curve and training time needed by the replacement employee to acclimate to the new environment and become familiar with management structures, processes, and procedures. Considering the time lost from the point that the initial incumbent was hired until the replacement incumbent is found, hired, and fully trained (sometimes a full year or better), the real cost of lost productivity to the terminating organization can be very significant indeed. Certainly nothing to take lightly!

All of this points to a need for both the hiring organization and the job seeker to pay particular attention to the matter of organizational compatibility. Both participants, during the interview process, must give this important issue the degree of attention necessary to ensure that the individual and the organization are fully compatible and that their employment relationship will endure.

As an interviewee, it is very important to include organization compatibility as part of your overall employment and interview strategy. We will now further explore the components of compatibility and, in doing so, try to help you develop a strategy that will prove helpful in gauging your compatibility and fit with prospective employer organizations.

There are two dimensions to organizational compatibility that need to be considered. The first is compatibility with the immediate work group. The second is compatibility with the organization as a whole. I will explore both of these dimensions thoroughly with you.

WORK GROUP COMPATIBILITY

How well will you fit with the immediate work group with whom you will be working? Will you feel comfortable and at home? Will you be readily accepted by the group and invited to participate, or will you be excluded from meaningful participation and made to feel an outsider?

Since this is the group with whom you will be working day in and day out, these are pretty important questions to be asking yourself as you prepare for your employment interview. After all, you will be dependent on members of your immediate work group for ideas and support. It's highly likely that incompatibility with this important group will quickly cause estrangement, lack of support, and eventual failure. Conversely, compatibility with this group will lead to early group acceptance, strong support, and a high probability of success.

ASSESSING WORK GROUP COMPATIBILITY

There is nothing magical about work group compatibility assessment. In fact, it is a fairly straightforward, logical approach using some careful observation and a lot of common sense. In general terms, it is a comparative method whereby one compares the overall profile of the work group with the profile of the individual to determine the degree of similarity or dissimilarity, and then uses this comparison to predict the probability of a successful fit.

Since there is a high likelihood that you may have only a short period of time with individual members of the group during the interview process, you will have a limited opportunity to gather information from which to construct an accurate or representative profile. This means that you must take some time to play your strategy in advance of the interview date.

A good place to start is when you are extended an opportunity to visit the employer for an interview. Ask the employer whether or not there will be an opportunity to meet with other members of the department with whom you would be working on a daily basis. Tell the employer that you consider this an important part of the interview process, and would like to meet with these people. Should time not allow for this during the initial interview, suggest to the employer that, should things go well during the first interview, and should there be mutual interest in pursing the matter further, perhaps a second interview might be arranged so that you would have an opportunity to meet with these employees prior to having to make an employment decision.

If the employer should balk at this suggestion, simply state that you feel it is very important to your decision that you have an opportunity to ascertain that you will feel at home and compatible with this group since you will need their help and you will be working closely together on a daily basis. If, at this point, such a request continues to fall on deaf ears, I suggest you question the interviewer's reluctance to have such a meeting take place. In the absence of a meaningful explanation, I seriously question whether this is the kind of organization for which you would like to work, and strongly suggest that you take your employment candidacy elsewhere.

In preparation for this meeting, there are a number of questions for which you will need answers in order to arrive at a reasonably accurate description of the group's profile. Here is a list to get you thinking about this subject:

1. What is the overall philosophy of the group?
2. What does the group consider important?
3. What do they consider unimportant?

4. How do they measure group success?

5. How do they measure group failure?

6. What do they believe it takes for an individual to be successful in their work unit?

7. Which are considered to be the most successful members of the work group? What has made them successful?

8. Who are the obvious leaders of the group? What is their work philosophy? What is their personal style? Are there similarities? Are there differences? What are they?

9. What makes the leaders different from the other unit members? In what ways are they similar?

10. What seem to be the predominant personality traits of successful group members? What adjectives can be used to best describe these individuals?

As you can see from the preceding list of questions, there is a lot of information to be gathered during the interview process which can prove exceedingly helpful in predicting your probable extent of compatibility with the work unit. Essentially, this information can be developed only through either observation or questions asked by you during the interview itself. A combination of both will be needed to gain a good understanding of the general operating environment in which you will need to function.

Here is a list of questions for use during the interview that should prove very helpful in defining organizational climate:

1. How would you describe the operating environment in which you work? What adjectives would you use to describe it?

2. In what ways is it the same or different from other environments in which you have worked?

3. What do you enjoy about the current work environment?

4. Conversely, what do you find frustrating? Why?

5. If there was something that you could change about the current work environment what would it be?

6. How would you change it? Why?

7. How would you categorize the management style and philosophy of this department? What adjectives would you use to describe it?

8. What factors determine the success of a person in this department?

9. Which are most valued?

10. What factors typically cause a person to fail in this environment?

11. Have there been such failures in the past? Why?

12. Could these failures have been avoided? How?

13. What other things can you tell me about the work environment of this department to help me better measure my overall compatibility with it?

These questions will arm you with considerable data for use in structuring a fairly accurate profile of the work group and environment in which you would be employed. The next step in this process is for you to construct a personal profile with which to compare the profile of the new environment. The following is a method to help you to structure such a personal profile.

PERSONAL PROFILE

It is recommended that you take the time to construct a personal profile well in advance of your first interview. This will assure prior objectivity and reduce the temptation for you to structure a personal profile out of excitement that is unrealistically compatible with that of the organization with which you will be interviewing. It is often very difficult to be totally objective about ourselves, but fortunately we frequently have some hard evidence in the way of past feedback from others that can help prevent us from engaging in self-delusion.

The most common source of such evidence are performance evaluations. Past performance evaluations represent observations of others about your personal style and characteristics. Another source is the "development needs/training needs assessment form," a document normally prepared by your supervisor. This document is used to determine your shortcomings—those areas in which you need further training and/or development to improve your performance capability.

An important, additional source of feedback concerning your personal traits and operating style are past intimate discussions that you have had on this subject with family members, fellow workers, and friends. If you try hard enough, you can probably think of additional sources of such personal feedback.

You will need to ask yourself a number of questions in order to construct a personal profile to compare with the employer's environment. You should find the following questions very helpful in this regard:

1. How would you describe yourself? What adjectives would you use?

2. How have others described you? What adjectives have they used to describe you?

3. Which past work environments have you enjoyed the most? Why?

4. Which past work environments have you least enjoyed? Why?

5. In which past work environments have you been most productive? Why?

6. What was characteristic of such environments?

7. In which past work environments have you been least productive? Why?

8. What was characteristic of such environments?

9. What is there about your personal profile (the kind of person that you are) that accounts for your success and professional satisfaction in a given environment?

10. What is there about your personal profile (the kind of person that you are) that has accounted for your past dissatisfaction or failure in a given environment?

11. How would you categorize your personal style and philosophy? What adjectives would you use to best describe this style and philosophy?

12. How would you describe your management style and philosophy? What adjectives would you use to best describe this style and philosophy?

13. What are your fundamental beliefs about what constitutes good management?

14. What is there about you that makes you believe these things?

15. How would you categorize the type of management environment in which you most like to work?

16. How would you categorize the type of management environment in which you would least like to work?

17. What is there about you that makes you feel this way about these environments?

As with the interview questions provided earlier in this chapter, these questions should arm you with considerable data about yourself from which to construct a fairly meaningful and informative profile.

COMPATIBILITY ASSESSMENT

You are now prepared to compare your personal profile with that of the organization with which you will be interviewing. This comparison should be a very effective tool for predicting the degree of compatibility (or incompatibility) with the prospective employer's organizational environment. The following sample profiles should help to make this point quite well.

PERSONAL PROFILE

Tends to be quiet, serious personality who enjoys working with others who appreciate thoroughness, professionalism, and accuracy. Am most productive in a professional environment that allows time for careful analysis in determining alternative courses of action. Am least comfortable in environments that are highly entrepreneurial, requiring fast decisions with little or no supportive data. Am a strong believer in participatory management where all members of the group are encouraged to input ideas. Am least happy in an authoritative, restrictive environment in which most decisions are made at the top.

ORGANIZATIONAL PROFILE

Organization is described as fairly unstructured and highly entrepreneurial. Successful persons are described as those who can make quick decisions with little or no supportive data available. Success is primarily measured by volume of productivity with only modest concern for quality of result. Past performance failures suggest that persons who have a need for extensive analysis as part of their decision-making process are usually not successful in this environment. Management style is described as highly authoritarian. Most decisions are made at the top.

Although the example is rather dramatic, it does make an important point about the importance of organizational compatibility as a key decision-making factor in the employment process. No matter how attractive the job may appear from the standpoint of technical challenge, scope, level of position, and so on, if your personal profile is not compatible with that of the hiring organization's work environment, there is a very high likelihood of failure. As you can see, then, organizational compatibility is an extremely important factor to consider in your employment decision process. It needs to be included as an important part of your employment interview strategy.

15

The Trend toward Competency-Based Interviewing

In recent years there has been a major trend toward the use of competency-based interviews as the preferred basis for candidate selection. As a job seeker, you need to be aware of this trend, and understand what is expected of you from the employer's perspective.

Before discussing competency-based interview tactics and techniques, you need an overall understanding of what competency-based interviews are and why they are taking on greater employer significance. The following overview should help you get a good grasp of this interview concept and enable you to better prepare for this increasingly popular interview technique.

WHAT IS A COMPETENCY?

Competencies, by definition, are the knowledge, skills, characteristics, and behaviors essential to successful performance of a given job.

THE JOB COMPETENCY MODEL

When preparing for an interview, employers who use competency-based interviewing start by first constructing a *job competency model*. The job competency model is simply a comprehensive profile of the competencies required for successful performance of the job.

WHY COMPETENCIES ARE IMPORTANT

Simply stated, competencies are the keys to organizational productivity and profitability.

In recent years, organizations have come to realize that there is a direct link between employees (human assets) and profit. This link is *competencies*. It is the overall competency level of the workforce that directly accounts for organizational success or failure.

Stated more specifically, it is people who plan, organize, control, and utilize all other assets of the business (i.e., capital, raw materials, equipment, technology, and human assets). How well employees plan and manage these business assets directly determines the success or failure of the enterprise. In other words, it is their level of competency that determines how effective they are in managing the firm's overall assets. If competence is high, the results are high productivity, effectiveness, and organizational success. On the other hand, if the overall competency level of the organization is low, the result is poor management of the company's resources and, in some cases, failure of the enterprise.

When needing to increase the overall competency and productivity of the organization, employers have increasingly come to realize there are only two ways by which this can be accomplished. These are employee selection and employee development. Hiring, selecting, and developing employees against the right set of competencies can, and will, play a major role in upgrading the overall efficiency and effectiveness of the organization.

Employers have come to appreciate that choosing employment candidates with the right competency set is critical to building a high-performing organization. Thus, they have now begun to focus more intensely on the best ways to define and measure

185

these important competencies when interviewing and selecting employment candidates.

Their awareness of the importance of competencies in employee hiring and selection has been further heightened as a result of several recent studies that clearly document the productivity and profitability gains that can be realized through the use of competency profiles in the hiring process. One such study, conducted by the American Psychological Association, for example, suggests employers can realize a 19 percent to 48 percent productivity gain (depending on level of job complexity) through use of valid job competency models to identify and select high-performing individuals with the right competency sets. Other studies of salesperson hiring suggest that such productivity gains can be in the range of 48 percent to 123 percent, depending on level of selling and type product sold. These impressive statistics have not escaped employer attention, as many have come to thoroughly embrace competency-based interviewing and selection as a means toward realization of substantial productivity gains for their organizations.

TYPES OF COMPETENCIES

Essentially there are two main categories of competencies: (1) technical competencies and (2) behavioral competencies. By definition, the term *technical competencies* means the specialized knowledge and skills essential to job success. The term *technical*, in this context, is not limited to just math and science. It is intended to cover *any* specialized knowledge or skills required to solve the key problems and achieve the expected results of a job.

The term *behavioral competencies,* on the other hand, means the personal traits, characteristics, and behaviors required for successful job performance.

Employers sometimes also distinguish between *threshold competencies* and *differentiating competencies.* Threshold competencies are those required for adequate job performance, while differentiating competencies are those that are uniquely common to only high-performing personnel in a given position. Since it is these differentiating competencies that distinguish between high-performing and nonhigh performing employees, employers have a particular interest in defining and measuring employment candidates against these high-performer attributes.

THE COMPETENCY-BASED INTERVIEW PROCESS

The process starts with the construction of a *job competency model.* This is a composite profile of the competencies important to successful job performance.

You may want to pay particular attention to the competency-modeling process and perhaps make use of this same system as a way to predict which competencies the employer is most likely to use when evaluating your candidacy for a given position. This will enable you to prepare, in advance, to answer questions related to the knowledge, skills, characteristics, and behaviors in which the employer is likely to have greatest interest. Careful analysis should enable you to identify an estimated 80 percent or better of these target competencies.

VALUE CHAIN ANALYSIS

The first step in job competency modeling is *value chain analysis.* Since the goal of most organizations is to continuously increase both productivity and profits, you must first determine in what ways the job for which you will be interviewing contributes to or impacts profitability. This is at the very essence of why the job exists. It must add value by directly or indirectly impacting the bottom line of the organization.

Here are some thought-stimulating questions that will help you zero in on the job's value proposition:

1. In what key ways does the job impact the overall productivity and profitability of the organization? List the top five or six.

   _____

   _____

   _____

   _____

   _____

   _____

   _____

2. What are the major opportunity areas for profit contribution by this position?

   _____

   _____

   _____

   _____

   _____

   _____

3. What are the expected results of the job from a productivity gain and profit standpoint?

   _____

   _____

   _____

   _____

   _____

   _____

   _____

DEFINING TECHNICAL COMPETENCIES

Now review the answers to the previous three questions for the
purpose of defining the key technical competencies required for
job success. What is the specialized knowledge and skill required
to successfully perform this job at a high level and maximize contribution to the overall productivity and profitability of the organization? List these in the spaces provided.

_____

_____

_____

_____

_____

_____

_____

_____

_____

Now, on a separate sheet of paper, force rank these competencies in the order of their importance, starting with those that have the greatest impact on organizational success and ending with those having least impact. Then, using a scale of 1 to 10 (10 high), rate each of these competencies based on their relative importance to success of the organization. Those that are critical and have major impact should be rated in the 8 to 10 range, those having moderate impact should be rated in the 5 to 7 range and, finally, those having minimal impact should be rated 1 to 4.

The net result of following this entire process is the identification and weighting of those technical competencies thought to be important to job success. The next step in the process is the definition and weighting of behavioral competencies.

DEFINING BEHAVIORAL COMPETENCIES

As previously explained, behavioral competencies are the personal traits, characteristics, and behaviors essential to high performance of a given position. The following two exercises should prove helpful in pinpointing some of the key personal attributes and behaviors required for a high level of job performance.

1. Review both the key results expected of the position as well as major opportunities to impact the overall productivity and financial results of the business, as defined in exercises you completed earlier in this chapter. Now, considering these factors, ask yourself, "What are the important personal characteristics and behaviors essential to job performance"? List these below.

(*Note:* To assist in this identification, I have provided a partial list of common personal traits and characteristics at the end of this chapter for your reference and review.)

_____

_____

_____

_____

_____

_____

Now, as with technical competencies, list these behavioral competencies on a separate sheet of paper in the order of their impact on job performance. Start your list with those competencies having greatest impact and end your list with those having least job performance impact.

2. Before assigning a rating to these behavioral competencies, perform one additional step. Think about people you have known and who you feel have been exceptional performers in this type of work. Then, list those behavioral attributes that distinguish these individuals from others (i.e., those personal traits and characteristics that have played a major role in their overall job success).

_____

_____

_____

_____

_____

_____

Next, compare this list of high-performer behavioral competencies to your previous listing of behavioral competencies. Add those not appearing on the original list, and then assign a rating to all competencies applying the same 1 to 10 rating scale used when rating technical competencies. Since these are the differentiating competencies (i.e., those distinguishing high performers from nonhigh performers), it should be obvious that they deserve the highest ratings (usually at the 8, 9, or 10 level).

FINALIZATION OF THE JOB COMPETENCY MODEL

The final step in the job competency modeling process is to combine the listing of weighted technical competencies with the weighted behavioral set to yield a complete model. Although a somewhat tedious process, if done thoughtfully, this process has probably enabled you to identify 80 percent or more of the key competencies against which you are to be measured by the employer.

BEHAVIORAL COMPETENCIES
COMMON TRAITS, CHARACTERISTICS, AND BEHAVIORS

Self-motivated	Energetic	Optimistic	Positive attitude
Confident	Self-assured	Open	Approachable
Friendly	Cordial	Sensitive	Empathetic
Objective	Open minded	Understanding	Candid
Direct	Diplomatic	Straightforward	Respectful
Self-composed	Honest	Principled	Trustworthy
Assertive	Aggressive	Adaptive	Flexible
Bold	Courageous	Daring	Risk taking
Persevering	Resilient	Tenacious	Persistent
Goal oriented	Results driven	Task oriented	Focused
Loyal	Dedicated	Hard working	Committed
Organized	Disciplined	Thorough	Accurate
Efficient	Proficient	Quality oriented	Client focused
Intelligent	Strategic	Independent	Thoughtful
Innovative	Creative	Analytical	Fair
Even handed	Insightful	Perceptive	Fast study
Participative	Team oriented	Group focused	Individualistic
Action oriented	Networker	Politically astute	Affable
Controlled	Unflappable	Values others	Values relationships
Persuasive	Convincing	Facilitative	Articulate
Negotiating	Dominating	Controlling	Commanding
Cautious	Careful	Thoughtful	Motivating

16

Surviving Behavior-Based Interviews

$\mathbf{I}$n Chapter 15 we discussed the rapidly growing trend of many U.S. companies toward competency-based interviewing. As we learned, firms using this approach are using job competency models as the basis for candidate interviewing and selection. And, as pointed out during this discussion, the first step in constructing a job competency model is the listing and weighting of those competencies, both technical and behavioral, required for successful job performance.

Once employers have defined these important selection criteria, the next step in their process is to develop *behavior-based interview questions*. Such questions are designed to enable employers to assess the competency level of prospective employment candidates against the critical competency set.

BEHAVIOR-BASED INTERVIEW QUESTIONS— MEASURING TECHNICAL COMPETENCIES

What is meant by a behavior-based interview question and, as a job candidate, how do you determine when the employer is using this type interview technique?

A behavior-based (or behavioral) interview question is one that is designed to determine what you will actually "do" when confronted with a particular situation or when asked to solve a given problem.

When attempting to measure your competency level with respect to a certain technical competency, employers typically will present you with a targeted problem and ask you to solve it. Such problems are carefully chosen so, when solving them, you will need to draw on specific knowledge felt by the employer to be critical to success in the job. In choosing this approach, the employer will be able to observe whether or not you have the appropriate knowledge, and whether you can successfully apply it.

For instance, if you were applying for a position as a corporate recruiter, typical behavioral questions you might be asked to measure technical competence as a staffing professional could include one or more of the following:

1. Assume a candidate's current annual salary is $75,000 and he or she tells you they require at least a 10 percent salary increase to seriously entertain an employment offer. Further, assume that the maximum base salary you are authorized to offer is $75,000. What would you do, and why?

2. A candidate has just turned down what you thought was a very competitive job offer. Disappointed with the offer rejection, the hiring manager tells you she really doesn't want to lose this candidate and asks you to see what you can do to reverse the candidate's decision. What would you do?

Both of these questions are designed to measure your technical competence (i.e., your specialized knowledge and skills) as a staffing professional. In the first example, the employer is attempting to measure your sales skills. The same question might also be employed to gauge competencies such as resourcefulness, creativity, and strategic thinking ability.

As a seasoned employment professional, it is expected that you would possess the specialized knowledge and skills required to successfully solve this problem. For example, some options you could cite, as evidence of your technical competence, might include:

1. Use of a signing bonus to sweeten the offer.
2. Use of a six-month salary review date, rather than the normal one-year review cycle.
3. Offer to pick up certain moving expenses in lieu of the higher starting salary.
4. Offer other attractive benefits (e.g., extra week of vacation) in the place of the higher compensation level.
5. Reference the key reasons the candidate previously cited for wanting to leave his or her current job and reinforce how the position being offered could remedy these issues and provide an increased level of job or career satisfaction.
6. Verbally reinforce those aspects of the new position that the candidate stated he or she found particularly interesting and/or appealing, thereby focusing the candidate's attention on the positive factors for making the career move.

Successfully answering this type of behavioral interview question requires you to demonstrate certain specialized, technical knowledge that only an experienced recruiter is likely to possess. Failure to cite some of these options might well suggest to the employer that your technical knowledge, as a recruiter, is somewhat limited and that you lack important qualifications for success in the job.

The second behavioral question, as with the first, requires the candidate to demonstrate his or her technical proficiency as an employment professional. A knowledgeable employment professional, for example, would know just what questions to ask a job candidate for the purpose of defining and clarifying the barriers standing in the way of offer acceptance. For example, a skilled recruiter might attack the problem this way in an effort to clarify these issues and convince the employment candidate to reverse his or her decision, and accept the job offer.

> John, I talked with Mary Joe (the hiring manager), and we are both quite disappointed that you elected to turn down our employment offer. We would very much like to have you come aboard here at the Volt Company and know, once on board, you would find the job and the work environment both rewarding and stimulating. Can you help us out here? What are the key reasons you decided to reject our offer, John, and what can we do to change your mind? We think you would make a great addition to the Finance Team, and would hate to lose this opportunity to have you join us.

As you can see, from the way this issue was addressed, our recruiter candidate is rather skilled in attempting to turn a rejected job offer around. You can see how he first attempted to build the candidate's ego by stating how much the company wanted the candidate to come aboard, making the candidate feel wanted and important. He then immediately attempted to clarify exactly what barriers stood in the way of getting offer acceptance. A lesser skilled candidate would probably not have a clue about how to successfully reverse an offer decision, and might start changing offer parameters without first identifying the real barriers standing in the way of job offer acceptance.

As a job seeker, you should now be able to clearly see just how effective well-designed behavior-based interview questions can be in measuring technical competencies. By simply citing a problem and asking you what you would do, the employer forces you to demonstrate the depth and breadth of your technical skills as a professional in your field. This is a highly effective interview technique that many employers are now using.

PREPARING FOR THE TECHNICAL SIDE OF THE BEHAVIORAL INTERVIEW

In preparing for the job interview, behavioral questions are, for the most part, the most difficult questions for which to prepare. This is because the situations or problems posed by the employer are practically limitless. In such cases, therefore, how can you possibly prepare for success in the interview? How can you anticipate the questions you are most likely to be asked?

When preparing for the technical side of the behavioral interview, you will need to think strategically — as if you are the employer attempting to design good behavior-based interview questions. At this point, a quick review of how employers define technical competencies (see Chapter 15, pages 186 to 187), should prove particularly beneficial in helping you to zero in on those technical competencies most likely to be targeted for evaluation by the employer.

Start by thinking about why the job exists. What key results are expected from this position? Having defined these results, then ask yourself what key problems you must successfully solve to achieve these results? Next, delineate the specialized knowledge and/or skills needed to successfully resolve these key issues.

Once you have identified the specialized knowledge and/or skills needed to address the key problems and challenges faced by the position, you are well on your way to preparing for the technical side of the job interview. There is a high likelihood that these very same problems (or ones similar to them) will be the focal point of most of the employer's behavior-based interview questions. Although the actual questions may vary, you can bet the ranch that almost all will be focused on measuring the same technical competency skill set.

You are now ready to begin practicing for the technical side of the interview. To do this, list the key problems you will be required to solve and the major challenges you are likely to face in the new position. Now practice describing what you would do to solve these key problems and achieve the results expected of the position. See how creative you can be by citing several different approaches and possible solutions to these problems.

When practicing your answers, be sure to focus on demonstrating the depth and breadth of your specialized knowledge and skills and cite how you would use these to achieve the desired results. It is also particularly convincing if you can cite specific examples of actual problems, similar to the one you are addressing, that required you to apply a high level of this knowledge and/or skill.

Then, as an additional strategy, once the actual interview begins, ask the hiring manager to identify some of the key problems you will face in the new position. Also ask the employer to describe the desired results and/or improvements he or she would like to see achieved. Questions of this type should help you to immediately zero in on what specialized knowledge and skills the employer considers important to job success. Highlighting these during the interview should provide you with a huge competitive advantage over other candidates who neglect to understand the priorities of the hiring manager.

Behavioral versus Technical Competencies

Employers are very much aware that certain personal traits, characteristics, and behaviors are essential to successful job performance. Collectively, these are known as *behavioral competencies*. Once they have determined you possess the technical knowledge and skills required for successful job performance, employers will quickly begin to focus much of their energy on measuring your behavioral competencies.

To exemplify behavioral competencies so that you have a better understanding, let's consider the position of Human Resource Manager. Most of you will be fairly familiar with this job.

It is generally acknowledged that successful human resource executives, as a group, typically exhibit certain personal traits and characteristics that contribute to job success. Some examples include:

- Open and approachable.
- Good listener.
- Sensitive to the feelings of others.
- Warm, cordial, friendly.
- Diplomatic.
- Effective communicator.

These are all behavioral traits or competencies that are considered important to success in this occupation. Persons lacking these desirable traits, although they may be technically competent, are unlikely to succeed in the field of human resources.

202

As another example, effective sales professionals generally possess certain behavioral traits and characteristics that contribute significantly to their selling ability. Some examples of these behavioral competencies typically include:

- Persuasiveness.
- Resilience.
- Persistence.
- Assertiveness.
- Skillful listener.
- Articulate.

It is hard to imagine that a person could be successful in sales without having a relatively high degree of these behavioral competencies. Conversely, it is hard to visualize a successful sales representative without them.

HOW EMPLOYERS MEASURE DESIRED BEHAVIORS

Employers use observation as the primary interview technique for assessing an employment candidate's behavioral competencies. For example, it would be difficult to think of interview questions that would be capable of measuring such behavioral skills and attributes as listening skills, articulation, warmth, friendliness, openness, approachability, and so on. Such behavioral competencies are typically measured through simple observation during the course of the job interview. Does the candidate exhibit these behavioral attributes during the interview or not? Exhibiting the desired behavioral traits during the interview will be important to your interviewing success.

There are other behavioral attributes, however, that employers will probe through use of good interview design. Using a sales position as our example, here are some illustrations:

1. Tell me about a time when your failure to listen carefully cost you a sale. What did you do?

   (*Comment:* An excellent question for assessing "listening skills.")

2. Describe a situation when careful listening really paid off for you.

   (*Comment:* Again, a good question for measuring "listening skills.")

3. Tell me about a time when you were told by a prospective customer that he or she had a close personal relationship with one of your competitors and would therefore not buy from you. What did you do?

   (*Comment:* An excellent question for assessing several behavioral competencies such as assertiveness, persistence, resilience, and/or persuasiveness.)

4. If your boss told you he or she didn't feel you were very thorough, but you disagreed, what would you do?

   (*Comment:* An effective question for measuring "assertiveness.")

You can see how effective these behavior-based questions are when used by employers to evaluate an employment candidate's competency level.

PREPARING FOR THE BEHAVIORAL SIDE OF THE BEHAVIOR-BASED JOB INTERVIEW

To begin preparation for the behavioral side of the job interview, you will need to identify those behaviors normally associated with high performers in the type position for which you are interviewing. The following questions should prove helpful in identifying such behavioral competencies, and in helping you successfully prepare for this type interview strategy:

1. What are the behaviors that distinguish high performers from others in this type work?

2. Why are these behaviors important?

3. Why are persons exhibiting these particular behaviors so successful in this type work?

4. Why are persons lacking these particular personal attributes typically unsuccessful (or less effective) in performing this type work?

5. In what way do you need to behave, during the interview, to demonstrate the desirable personal attributes sought by employers for this type position?

6. What type behavior should you avoid?

7. What type behavior do you need to emphasize?

In preparation for the interview, I now suggest you make two lists. One should be headed "Desired Behaviors" and the other "Undesired Behaviors." Having completed these lists, have a friend run you through several mock job interviews, scoring you each time against both the desired and undesired behaviors contained on your lists. Have the friend record a checkmark beside each type behavior, both desired and undesired, each time that behavior is evident during the course of the interview. At the conclusion, by observing the pattern of these checkmarks, you should be able to quickly see where you need to modify your behavior to ensure interview success. Ask your friend for advice and ideas on how you might be more effective in highlighting the desired behaviors during the interview. Try this mock interview process with other friends and/or family members until you are confident that you are effectively exhibiting the positive behaviors for which prospective employers will be looking.

Videotaping these interviews can also prove extremely effective as a coaching tool. Videotape playback of these mock interviews, coupled with self-evaluation and the coaching by others, should help you make the necessary behavioral modifications important to making a good impression during the job interview.

Now, taking the same list of desirable behavioral attributes, pick those that can be best probed through use of well-designed behavioral interview questions. Try your hand at designing a series of behavior-based interview questions similar to those illustrated below. To be sure your practice questions are truly behavior-based, try starting each question with the introductive statements shown below:

1. Tell me about a time when _____ . What did you do?

   Example: Tell me about a time when your persuasiveness really paid off. What happened, and what did you do?

   Example: Tell me about a time when you had a good idea but were unable to persuade your boss. What did you do?

206

2. Describe a time when _____ . What did you do?

   Example: Describe a time when you needed to be particularly assertive. What did you do, and what was the outcome?

   Example: Describe a time when your honesty proved very important. What happened, and what did you do?

   Example: Describe a time when someone questioned your honesty. What did you do?

3. Tell me about a time when you failed to _____ . What happened, and what did you do?

   Example: Tell me about a time when your failure to focus on details caused a problem. What did you do?

   Example: Tell me about a time when your failure to pay attention to someone's feelings caused them to get angry at you. What happened? What did you do?

Citing times when your use of a particular behavioral attribute led to a positive result is the easy part of interview preparation. Citing times when your failure to employ a certain behavioral attribute led to a specific problem, however, creates a far more difficult challenge for the job seeker. The best way to prepare for this eventuality, however, is to cite an example where the initial outcome appeared potentially disastrous, but you were able to salvage the situation and realize a positive outcome. Doing so will demonstrate your skill and creativity rather than to leave the employer with the impression that you lacked the necessary skill and imagination to convert a bad situation into a positive result.

Using the list of desired behaviors as the basis for designing behavior-based interview questions and then practicing your answers is about the only way to successfully prepare for the behavioral interview. You can be sure that many employers will use this type interview format, so it is best to spend the necessary time to be well prepared.

17

Questions You'll Need to Ask

The employment interview is designed to be a two-way conversation that is intended to provide for a maximum flow of information in both directions, so that both parties have sufficient information on which to base a well-founded employment decision. It is the employer's goal to have sufficient information about the candidate's qualifications, including such things as education, experience, knowledge, skills, personal style, and so on. The candidate, on the other hand, needs information in a number of categories such as company background, department, job, work environment, promotional opportunities, and compensation. Therefore, it is important that the interview provide an environment that will allow for a balanced flow of information between both parties so that an intelligent employment decision can be made.

Generally speaking, control of the interview process rests with the hiring organization. The employer should be sensitive to this need for good balance and should plan the interview so that you will have ample opportunity to ask those questions that will be important to your employment decision.

It is possible that you will encounter inexperienced interviewers who are not as sensitive as they should be. You may, for example, run into the "interrogator"—the interviewer who is so absorbed in asking about you and your background that there is little or no opportunity for you to ask about the job or the company. On the other hand, you may encounter the "company loyalist"— the individual who is so interested in telling you about the company and the job that he or she neglects to ask you important questions concerning your qualifications for the position.

It is important that you be sensitive to this need for a good balance between getting and giving information, and that you do what you can to effect a proper balance. This may mean occasionally interceding in an effort to redirect the flow of information. There are some methods for doing this which we will discuss shortly.

Should you decide to intercede in the interview process, be sure that your intrusion is well-timed. This is particularly true when it comes to interrupting the interviewer's questions about you and your background. To interrupt this process before the employer has had time to develop sufficient information on which to formulate a hiring decision can seriously jeopardize your employment chances. Remember that your first priority during the interview is to generate sufficient interest so that the employer will be inclined to hire you. Should you fail to achieve this first objective, the interview, as well as the employment opportunity, could well be lost. Also, remember that you will likely have ample opportunity to ask your questions during a second visit or by phone following receipt of an actual offer of employment.

Nevertheless, should it be clear that the employer has had the opportunity to thoroughly explore your background, and if you perceive that the interview is beginning to float into areas not really related to core qualifications (e.g., hobbies, extracurricular activities), you should make an attempt to intervene and redirect the flow of the discussion to focus on those areas that are of interest to you. You can do so firmly and politely by using one of the following lead-in statements:

1. Mr. Cruthers, if you will excuse the interruption, there are some areas of importance to me that I would like to explore. Would you mind if we talk a little further about the position?

2. Perhaps before we get into these areas, Mr. Cruthers, could we talk a little more about the position? Would you mind?

3. In the interest of time, Mr. Cruthers, perhaps we could talk further about the position. Do you mind?

You will note that the wording of these intervention statements leaves ultimate control of the interview in the hands of the interviewer. Should the interviewer feel that he or she has sufficient information about you to arrive at an employment decision, he or she will probably agree to this change in direction. Conversely, should it be felt that additional information is needed, the interviewer will politely suggest that you continue along the original line of questioning. However, in such cases, the employer will normally acknowledge your need for more information and will offer to cover these areas later, either by phone or during a second interview.

Regardless of when these questions are asked, there are a number of key questions that you should consider asking the employer either during or following the initial interview. The following is a list of such questions arranged by category. Note that this list does not include the key strategic questions which were discussed earlier. These were excluded intentionally, since I've assumed that you have already carefully read these previous chapters.

THE COMPANY

Wherever possible, you should secure and read a copy of the company's annual report in advance of your interview.

1. What are the prospects for future growth and expansion of the company?

2. What new products is the company planning to introduce that will support future growth?

3. What new markets is the company considering entering that are in line with growth plans?

4. Is the company considering ventures or acquisitions as part of its growth plan?

5. If so, in what areas?

6. Are these related to existing products and/or markets, or are they intended for diversification?

7. What has accounted for fluctuations in sales (or profits) over the last _____ years?

8. What kind of annual growth rate do you expect to see over the next 5 to 10 years? Why?

9. Has the organization had any layoffs or cutbacks in the last 5 years?

10. If so, how many employees and what groups were affected?

11. Was this group affected? How? To what degree?

12. Are any employee cutbacks planned or anticipated in the foreseeable future?

13. What effect, if any, would you expect these to have on this position and/or department?

THE DEPARTMENT/FUNCTION

Sample questions regarding the department/function include:

1. How is the current department/function organized?

2. What are the overall functional responsibilities?

3. What organizational changes do you anticipate? Why?

4. What are the major challenges and objectives currently faced by the department/function?

5. What future challenges and new objectives do you anticipate?

6. How is this department/function viewed by others in the organization? Why?

7. What are the major opportunities for the department/function to improve its overall contribution to the organization?

THE JOB

Frequently asked questions about the job are:

1. Why is the position open?

2. Is it a new position or was there a prior incumbent?

   a. If newly created position:

      Why was position created?

      What factors led to this decision?

   b. If prior incumbent:

      Where did past incumbent go?

      If promoted, where and when?

      If transferred, where and when?

      If resigned, why?

      If fired, why? In what ways did performance fall short?

3. Why isn't this position being filled from within the company?

4. To whom does this position report?

5. Are any changes in reporting relationship anticipated? If so, why?

6. What are the names and titles of those individuals reporting directly to this position?

7. What positions report to this job indirectly (through others)?

8. What are the functional responsibilities of this position?

9. What are the quantitative dimensions of the position (number of persons managed, budgets, sales volume, cost of goods manufactured, etc.)?

10. What are the key ongoing responsibilities of this position?

11. Are there any changes expected in these responsibilities? If so, what, why, and when?

12. Other than these ongoing responsibilities, is this position responsible for meeting any special objectives? If so, what are they? What is the status of each?

13. With what other key individuals or groups does this position interface?

14. What is the nature of this relationship?

15. What opportunities exist to bring about improvement in the performance of this position?

16. What improvement would you like to see in these areas?

17. What key problems or barriers have prevented progress in these areas in the past?

PERFORMANCE EVALUATION

Questions regarding performance evaluation include:

1. Is there a formal performance evaluation system?
2. What is the basis for measuring employee performance? What criteria are used?
3. How does the performance evaluation system work?
4. How frequently are performance evaluations done?
5. Is there input into this system by persons other than the immediate supervisor? If so, by whom?
6. What opportunity is there for employee input?
7. What form does this performance evaluation take?
8. If an employee disagrees with the evaluation, what options are available to express this disagreement?

ADVANCEMENT OPPORTUNITIES

Advancement opportunities should be discussed. Questions to ask include:

1. Assuming good performance, how long might I expect to be in this position?
2. To what positions would I likely progress? Why?
3. What other options might be available?
4. What factors are used to determine promotion eligibility?
5. Who were the last three persons to have held this position?
6. Where are they now?

7. Who was in the position for the shortest time? Why?

8. Who was in this position for the longest period of time? Why?

9. Is there any reason why, assuming good performance, I should expect to be in this position for an extended period of time? If so, approximately how long? Why?

10. What training and development is provided to the employee to help prepare for future promotion and advancement?

11. Are there formal training programs available? How do these work?

12. Does the company support additional formal education? What form does such support take?

13. Is there an educational refund program? If so, how does it work?

14. What else can you tell me about opportunities for promotion and advancement?

COMPENSATION

Questions regarding compensation should be discussed during the interview. Examples are:

1. Does the company have formal salary ranges for given jobs?

2. How are these salary ranges determined?

3. What is the salary range of this position?

4. Is there a formal salary review program? If so, how does it work?

5. How often are employee salaries reviewed?

6. What is used as the basis for determining the amount of such increases?

7. What is the typical range of these increases?

8. Other than routine reviews, are there any other kinds of salary increases?

9. What circumstances warrant such increases?

10. What is the basis for determining the amount of such increases?

11. What is the typical amount of such increases?

12. Does this position qualify for any form of incentive income? If so, what is the nature of such income?

13. What is the basis for determining the amount of incentive payments?

14. How often are such payments made?

15. What has normally been the magnitude of these payments?

16. Are there any other forms of compensation? If so, what are they and how do they work?

BENEFITS

It is important that you not take up valuable interview discussion time discussing benefits. Usually, the employer will have a written summary of the company's benefits that can be made available to you for the asking. If the following questions are not answered by reading this summary, and there is reason to believe that the employer has strong interest in your employment candidacy, you should ask to speak with someone in the personnel department to secure answers to your remaining questions.

1. What insurance benefits are provided by the company?
   a. Life insurance?
   b. Hospitalization?
   c. Surgical?
   d. Major medical?
   e. Disability?
   f. Dental?
   g. Other?
2. What is the extent of these coverages?
3. What will be your costs for carrying these coverages?
4. Which of these insurances provide for dependent coverage?
5. What are the costs for such coverages? Are they paid by the company, the employee, or both?
6. Is there a retirement plan? If so,
   a. Is it contributory or noncontributory?
   b. What is the employee's contribution amount?
   c. What is the retirement benefit amount?
7. Is there a profit sharing program? If so, how does it work and what has been recent payout history?
8. Is there a 401K plan? If so, how does it work?
9. Is there a savings and investment plan? If so, how does it work?

10. Is there paid sick leave? If so, how does it work?

11. Is there a tuition refund plan? If so, how does it work?

12. Are there company paid holidays? What are they?

13. What is your vacation policy? How does it work?

14. What other benefits does the organization provide? Describe.

Moving Expenses

As with benefits, it is not advisable to become involved in a discussion about moving expenses during an initial interview. This will only take up valuable time that could be put to better use. However, once it is clear that the company is intending to make an employment offer to you, it is very important that you gain a clear understanding concerning those moving expenses for which you can be reimbursed by the employer. Such expenses can be very substantial, so it is important that you know which ones you will personally be responsible for.

1. Reimbursement of sale closing costs? (Sale of old location house.)

2. Reimbursement of purchase closing costs? (Purchase of new location house.)

3. Assistance in sale of old location house? (Explain.)

4. Protection on sale price of old location house? (Extent?)

5. Are real estate equity loans available (if needed to make down payment on new location house)? Basis and terms?

6. If renting, reimbursement of rental release fee or balance of lease payments (if no release can be obtained)?

7. House hunting trip (with spouse)?

8. Temporary living expenses (with family)? Limitations?

9. Shipment of household goods?

10. Storage of household goods (if necessary)?

11. Final trip to new location (with family)?

12. Tax gross up of taxable portion of moving expense reimbursement? (The IRS considers certain moving expense reimbursements by the employer to constitute taxable income for federal income tax purposes.)

THE RESIDENTIAL AREA

Here again, it is not advisable to take up valuable interview time to discuss the area. There should be ample time to collect much of this information after the interview, should there be strong interest in your employment candidacy. Nonetheless, it is important to gather certain information about the area in which you will be living. In particular, you will need to have a good understanding of living costs in the new area if you are to be in a good position to evaluate the financial aspects of any employment offer made to you. The following is intended as a checklist for asking the employer about such costs in the new area:

1. Housing or rental costs?

2. Mortgage costs?

3. Real estate taxes?

4. Homeowners insurance?

5. Utility costs:
   a. Heat?
   b. Water?

c. Electricity?

    d. Gas?

6. State income taxes?

7. Local income taxes (county, city, township)?

8. Personal property taxes?

9. Other assessments or taxes? Explain.

10. Food?

11. Clothing?

12. Automobile insurance?

13. Commuting costs?

Beyond the cost items listed here, there may be many other questions you may wish to ask, depending on your personal interests, hobbies, and marital status. It is advisable to make a list of these items if they are important to you, so that you don't neglect to collect information about them at some stage in the interview and employment process.

18

Interview Tips—
Do's and Don'ts

The following is a list of suggestions for proper preparation for, and decorum during, the employment interview. These tips should be well-heeded, as many of them deal with aspects of planning and appearance that can have a significant effect on your presentation, and very possibly your chances of being hired.

Always collect as much information as possible about the company and position before the interview. Where available, this should include:
>   Annual report
>   Position description
>   Position objectives, current year
>   Business plan

Where time allows (and if the position is of particularly strong interest to you) spend some time in the library to research the company. Some good sources include:
>   Industry journals
>   Industry directories
>   Trade publications
>   Dun & Bradstreet's *Million Dollar Directory*
>   Standard & Poor's *corporation records, reports,* and stock index
>   *Value Line*
>   You might also consult your stockbroker.

Get plenty of sleep the night before the interview so that you will feel fresh and alert.

Eat a hearty breakfast so that you will feel satisfied and have plenty of reserve energy on which to draw as you need it. But don't overeat, since this could cause you to feel drowsy and listless.

Be punctual. You should plan your time so that you arrive at least 5 to 10 minutes ahead of time. A last-minute arrival will cause you to feel tense and uneasy. You will want to feel relaxed and confident as you enter the interview.

Dress properly. Be sure your clothes are clean and neatly pressed. Shoes should be well shined. Avoid wearing outlandish styles or colors. Dress appropriately for the position and organization with which you will be interviewing. In most cases, for men, a dark blue or grey business suit with white shirt and an appropriately colored tie will serve you well. For women, the choice is much broader, but should be guided by conservative colors and good taste.

Pay attention to personal hygiene and grooming. Hair (including mustaches and beards) should be neatly trimmed and combed. Hands and fingernails should be clean. Perfume and cologne should be used with moderation and should not overpower the interviewer.

Don't smoke, chew gum, or eat during the interview. This can detract substantially from your presentation and overall image.

Be polite, courteous, and friendly to the interviewer's support staff (i.e., secretary, administrative assistant, assistant). These individuals will frequently relay their impressions of an employment candidate to their supervisor.

When greeting the interviewer, be pleasant; smile, extend a firm (but not crushing) handshake, and look him or her in the eye. Do not sit until asked.

Maintain eye contact throughout the interview. Occasionally look away, at appropriate moments, so that your host does not feel challenged to a staring contest.

Be alert to your body language throughout the interview. Be careful not to slouch down in the chair. This may be interpreted negatively by the interviewer (i.e., you are disinterested in what is being said, you are lazy or sloppy, you are not concerned with your personal appearance). Conversely, do not sit rigidly or on the edge of the chair. If too rigid, you may project the image of someone who is overly formal, unfriendly, or distant. Likewise, sitting on the edge of the chair may make you appear nervous, anxious, high strung, or overly aggressive. Maintain good posture and a relaxed, but attentive, demeanor throughout the interview.

Gesticulate appropriately to make a key point. However, be careful not to overgesticulate, since this can draw the interviewer's attention away from what you are saying and can detract substantially from your overall presentation.

Avoid unnecessary fidgeting with your hands or fingers, such as tapping your fingers, playing with pencils and paper clips, stroking your beard or hair, pulling your ear, rubbing your nose, and so on. All of these suggest nervousness and will distract interviewers, thereby causing them to pay less attention to what you are saying.

Be pleasant, friendly, warm, and polite throughout the interview. Remember to smile from time to time. You'll want to establish and maintain good personal rapport with the interviewer throughout the discussion.

Be careful not to dominate the interview discussion. This can cause the interviewer to feel anxious, or even hostile. Be sensitive to the interviewer's right to control the interview, and do your part to ensure a well-balanced, two-way exchange of information.

Never volunteer negative information to the interviewer. However, should such information come to light as a result of the interviewer's questioning, don't dodge the issue. Be factual and honest, but be brief! Try to present this information in as positive a light as possible, but don't overexplain or apologize.

Observe the interviewer's body language. This can often indicate how well the interview is going. A smile or nod of the head can tell you that you are on the right track and your host agrees with what you are saying. If your host begins to shift from side to side, play with a pencil, or look away, this may signal lack of interest and tell you that you need to move on. A scowl or frown may signal that the interviewer disagrees with what you are saying.

Use your interviewing techniques to ferret out those areas of particular interest to the interviewer. Watch for signs of unusual interest or excitement. Spend some time to exploit this interest and satisfy your host's curiosity.

Use your interview techniques to discover the employer's hot buttons—those issues that are key to the employer's hiring decision. Use these to frame yourself as the ideal candidate who can bring improvement and add value to the organization in these important areas.

Use the five-minute interview strategy to focus on the strategic needs of the employer. This will enable you to position yourself as a positive change agent who can help the organization to achieve its strategic objectives, thus adding value to the organization.

Use the voids strategy (Chapter 10) to position yourself as someone who can fill current job and performance voids, and add value to the organization.

If you are interested in the position, tell the employer of your interest before the conclusion of the interview. Ask the employer for some feedback.

Thank the interviewer for his or her time and ask when you can expect to hear from them.

Write a brief "thank you" letter after the interview. This should thank the interviewer for their time and also restate your interest in the position.

Take time after the interview to critique your own performance. What areas of the interview went well? How could these have been further strengthened? What aspects of the interview didn't go that well? What specifically went wrong? What could you do to improve your presentation in these areas? Use this information to better prepare yourself for your next employment interview discussion.

19

Resumes That
Win Interviews

Having a well-prepared, hard-hitting resume can do wonders for your interview effectiveness and job search results. Far too many job seekers hurriedly throw together a resume and run off to the job interview expecting they will do well. The results can often be disappointing if not disastrous.

You will find, in many cases, employers rely heavily on the resume as a focal point for the interview discussion. Many interviewers, in fact, use the resume as an interview guidepost, systematically working their way through your background, one job at a time. They will query you about your job title, reporting relationship, size and scope of the position you held, as well your functional responsibilities and key accomplishments.

A well-organized resume will make it easy for the interviewer to review your overall credentials and quickly understand where you've been and what you have done. This leaves much more time for the employer to focus on those specific skills and accomplishments of greatest interest that will most influence the hiring decision. On the other hand, if the resume is poorly organized, employers will waste far too much time looking for basic information, leaving less time to explore the knowledge, skills, and abilities most critical to job success.

If resume organization or format is so important to job interview success, what is the best format for the job seeker to use?

RESUME FORMAT

Over the years there has been considerable debate over what constitutes an effective resume format. If you haven't already, take time to browse the numerous resume books in the career section of your favorite bookstore and you will come away with your head spinning from the huge variety of resumes formats and styles recommended by various authors.

Unfortunately, many authors of resume books lack credible credentials and, although meaning well, provide a plethora of misguided information that can serve to undermine an otherwise carefully planned job-hunting campaign. It seems today that almost anyone who has conducted a job search can suddenly become a self-proclaimed expert on resume preparation. It is clear that the shelves of bookstores are piled high with books written by such self-proclaimed experts, and there is little to separate the wheat from the chaff.

As someone who has spent better than 30 years in the human resources field and hired hundreds of individuals, it would seem to me that the best source of resume advice is employment professionals, those who have spent years actually reading resumes and interviewing job candidates. Since these are clearly the experts whom your resume must impress, you will want to heed their advice and avoid the many would-be experts whose ability to use the computer to craft a sentence is about their only qualification to render professional employment advice.

ADVICE FROM EMPLOYMENT EXPERTS

Although I am a heavily experienced employment professional and have authored 12 best-selling job-hunting books, I think it is important to share not only my own opinion on resume preparation but also to support my recommendations with advice from other knowledgeable experts in the staffing field.

A good source for solid information regarding employment matters is the Employment Management Association (EMA). The EMA is a professional emphasis subgroup of the Society for Human Resource Management (SHRM), and is comprised of hundreds of employment professionals from a wide variety of companies and professional staffing firms. The EMA is widely recognized as the preeminent professional association to which staffing professionals belong and is highly regarded as the major authoritative source when it comes to expert opinion pertaining to employment matters.

In 2000, SHRM published an extensive survey on resumes and cover letters entitled *SHRM 2000 Cover Letters and Resume Survey*. This study was sent to 2,500 randomly selected members of the EMA, with some 582 human resource professionals responding. A copy of the full survey can be ordered directly from the SHRM Store by calling (800) 444-5006 (Item # 62.17032). I occasionally reference this study to further validate several of the resume recommendations I will be making with regard to effective resume writing.

Reverse Chronological Resume—The Preferred Resume Style

By far, the most popular resume format, and the one most preferred by employment professionals, is the reverse chronological resume. Although this has been widely acknowledged by employment experts for quite some time, the EMA survey documents that some 74 percent of human resource respondents view this particular format favorably. It is the most universally preferred and accepted resume style for use by job seekers.

The reverse chronological resume format (see pages 260 and 261) lists jobs in reverse chronological order, displaying the most recently held position first. This is followed by the second most recently held position, then the third most recently held position, and so on, with the last position shown on the resume being the first job held by its author.

It should stand to reason that employers are most interested in knowing about positions recently held, since these reflect your most current skills and abilities. Since these jobs highlight your most saleable qualifications, they deserve to be showcased at the very beginning of your resume document. With rare exception, positions held 10 or 15 years ago are of considerably less interest to the employer and, thus, do not deserve prime billing. Such positions should clearly be reserved for inclusion on the second or perhaps even third page of your resume.

SINGLE VERSUS MULTIPAGE RESUME?

Over the years, there has been considerable debate about the proper length of a resume. For some reason there is a prevalent myth that has persisted for a number of years suggesting that a resume should never exceed a single page in length. Quite frankly, this is hogwash!

Although it is true that job seekers with only three or four years of experience should strive to produce a single-page document, those who have held two or more positions, or have several years of experience, should feel free to spill over onto a second page. In fact, according to the EMA survey, some 91 percent of human resource professionals find two-page, single-sided resumes quite acceptable.

Be careful, however, not to overdo it! Although, on rare occasions, it may be necessary to include a third page to your resume, this is not recommended. If you find it absolutely necessary to do so, however, make sure that you don't fill the entire third page of the document. This will distract from your candidacy. Keeping it to a quarter page or at worst no more than a half page is strongly recommended!

The EMA survey shows 62 percent of employers view resumes of greater than two pages in length negatively and would much prefer a shorter resume document. There are probably two good reasons for this. First, busy employers already have too many resumes to read and don't have time to wade through a lengthy document to glean the candidate's most relevant qualifications. Second, there is normally little or no interest in positions held several years ago, so why spell these out in detail? Simply showing employer name, job title, and employment dates on these earlier-held positions is all that is necessary.

DEVELOPING THE REVERSE CHRONOLOGICAL RESUME

Although there are some slight variations, there appear to be some fairly uniform standards when it comes to formating the reverse chronological resume document. The standard resume layout normally includes the following four sections, which are almost universally presented on the resume in the order shown:

1. Resume Heading.
2. Profile (sometimes called Summary or Qualifications Summary).

3. Professional Experience.

4. Education.

Although these four sections should be considered mandatory, there are three additional resume sections that are commonly added following Education. These added sections, however, are optional and include:

5. Professional Memberships.

6. Patents (show relevant patents only).

7. Recognition and Awards.

Despite the fact that the recommended resume formating normally shows Education as the fourth section of the resume, there are some circumstances that dictate that the Education section be positioned third, just after Profile. If your education or degree is relatively recent and is relevant to the position for which you are applying, it is recommended that you position it just after the Profile section of your resume. Additionally, if your degree is from a prestigious school, considered a leading institution in the field for which you are applying, then, by all means, highlight this qualification by positioning it as the third item on your resume, directly following Profile. However, if you received your degree several years ago, you might not want to highlight your age by positioning this fact at the beginning of your resume. In such cases, you will want to downplay your age by positioning Education as originally recommended (i.e., after Professional Experience).

THINGS TO EXCLUDE FROM YOUR RESUME

There are certain things that should be excluded from your resume document and for good reason. These include:

1. Hobbies (unless directly relevant to job qualifications).

2. Extracurricular Activities (unless directly relevant to job qualifications).

3. Religious Affiliations (unless applying for a position in the field of religion).

4. Political Affiliations (unless applying for a position in the field of politics).

5. Racially-Oriented Affiliations (unless directly relevant to position you seek).

6. Personal Data (i.e., age, height, weight, marital status, medical data, etc.).

Employers are simply not interested in extraneous data that has little or no relevance to the position for which you are applying, so the best advice is to exclude these items from your resume entirely! They serve no practical purpose and may, in fact, distract from your overall qualifications reducing or eliminating further interest in your employment candidacy.

CONSTRUCTING AN EFFECTIVE REVERSE CHRONOLOGICAL RESUME

To assist you in writing an effective reverse chronological resume, I will systematically walk through each key resume section (as outlined above), starting with the resume Heading. Before we start, however, I recommend you take a few moments to carefully study the sample resume on pages 260 and 261, so that you will have an overall understanding of both the layout and general content normally incorporated into an effective reverse chronological resume document. As I describe each resume section, I will also incorporate an example so that you can visually see the key elements and relate them to the sample resume contained on page 261.

SECTION 1—HEADING

Before beginning a description of the resume Heading, a few words are needed about type fonts to be used throughout the resume document. The best advice here is too stick with standard, commonly used fonts such as *Times New Roman, Times Roman,* or *Arial.* Avoid use of fancy script, bold block, or other unusual type styles that may prove distracting to the reader. Except as noted, stay with 11 or 12 point as your type size.

The resume Heading typically includes five components:

1. Name.
2. Address.
3. Home Phone.
4. Cell Phone.
5. E-mail Address.

Take a moment to carefully study the following sample resume Heading, as well as the Heading shown on the sample resume (see page 260).

DAVID B. BRADFIED

125 East Main Street		(315) 552-7963 Home
Wilmington, NC 17456	*Davbrad@AOL.com*	(315) 473-9546 Cell

As illustrated in the above example, you will want to employ 12-point type size for the entire Heading. Since you will also want your name to stand out from the rest of the script, however, it is recommended that you use boldface type. Additionally, it is also recommended that you capitalize all letters of your name. You can readily see the effect this creates from the sample resume Heading.

To add some contrast and interest to the resume Heading, I suggest using italics when typing your e-mail address as done in the sample Heading.

SECTION 2—PROFILE

The Profile section of the resume document is generally the section where there is the most disagreement among employment professionals. Two other commonly used titles for this resume section are *Qualifications Summary* or simply *Summary*. It is your choice as to which title you prefer to use. Any of the three options is perfectly acceptable and makes very little difference to the average resume reader.

For the most part, there are two schools of thought among the experts concerning best use of this resume section by the job seeker. I will present both viewpoints here, and then provide my own thoughts on how to get the most mileage from this resume component.

Approach 1—Summary of Level and Type of Experience

According to one school of thought, the Profile section of the resume document is best used to provide a brief summary of the author's level and type of experience. If well-crafted, proponents of this approach believe it will serve two purposes.

First, it will grab the reader's attention by providing just enough information to determine the author's key qualifications without the need to read the entire resume. Without such a summary, supporters of this approach argue, the reader will be forced to read much of the resume document to ascertain whether or not the job applicant has the basic qualifications being sought. Many won't bother! They will simply move on to the next resume in the stack.

Second, many proponents believe by using the Profile section to provide an interesting portrayal of the job seeker's level and type of experience, the reader will feel compelled to actually read the full resume document.

Approach 2—Key Word Highlighting

Advocates of this approach argue that the use of certain key words in the Profile section will immediately grab the reader's attention, generating sufficient interest to compel the employer to read the balance of the resume document. Additionally, proponents argue that many employers electronically scan or import resumes via the Internet, then use keyword search technology to automatically identify prospective candidates by keying in on only those resumes containing the designated key words selected by the employer.

Although it is true that an increasing number of employers are using keyword search technology to identify desirable candidates, the use of automated keyword search is still pretty much in its infancy. For example, according to the EMA survey, some 88 percent of employers still screen resumes manually rather than rely on electronic means. Thus, the keyword search argument does not seem to be well supported by survey results. It also suggests that the majority of employers do not believe that automated keyword search is a reliable method for identifying qualified candidates.

A further complicating factor to consider when using the re-sume Profile section to highlight certain key words is choosing the right words to include. How do you know what specific items to highlight? Is it certain personal traits and characteristics? Is it specific skills and competencies? Is it a certain type or level of experience? Is it experience working in a particular type of work environment? Is it experience with specific industries, with particular products, with certain processes, with specific markets? How do you decide which of these factors to highlight? If you choose one to the exclusion of another, could this automatically eliminate further consideration of your employment candidacy? If you choose to emphasize certain factors not of interest to a given employer, will this automatically screen you out?

As you can see, use of the resume's Profile section to highlight or emphasize certain of your qualifications is truly a "hit-or-miss" proposition. By selecting only certain factors, you may be excluding other qualifications in which the employer may have a great deal of interest. To use the Profile section in this fashion is akin to playing the employment equivalent of Russian roulette.

Approach 3 — A Balanced Approach

Although I cannot cite specific survey data to support this recommendation, in my judgment, the Profile section of the resume document should be a blend of Approaches 1 and 2. It should reflect level and type of experience but also include certain key words that best describe what you consider to be your strongest technical functional and personal attributes. This serves the employer's need by highlighting the level and type of experience sought. It also serves your personal needs by facilitating your selection for positions which are a good match for your personal profile and natural preferences.

The following are some examples of some well-written *Profile* statements:

Example 1

Profile

Skilled Marketing Manager with proven ability to successfully develop and lead specialty and industrial chemical businesses to profitable market growth. Expertise in strategic planning, competitive analysis, and new product development leading to significant revenue growth. Superior leadership, team building, customer relationship, and presentation skills.

Example 2

Profile

Talented mechanical Project Engineer with five years experience in the successful design, installation, and start-up of tissue and towel paper machines. Strong project management skills with excellent reputation for bringing projects in on time and under budget. Exceptional communication and interpersonal skills.

Example 3

Profile

Senior Sales Executive with proven history of establishing brands as the premiere market leader in the highly competitive consumer products industry. Reputation for developing exceptional, motivated sales teams who consistently exceed sales goals and build a strong, loyal customer base. Expertise in both the food and personal product sectors.

Review of these three examples shows that the word *Profile* is set in 12-point type, while accompanying text uses 11-point type. This treatment provides good visual separation of resume elements and enhances resume appearance as well as ease of reading. You might also want to "justify" margins, as shown, to avoid ragged edges and dangling text that distracts from overall resume appearance.

SECTION 3—PROFESSIONAL EXPERIENCE

The third resume component is Professional Experience section. This is the guts of the resume document and serves to highlight your specific employment experience. Since we are designing a reverse chronological resume, this section of the resume document begins with your current or most recently held position. It then continues to systematically highlight each previously held position, going back in time, such that your first job is the last position listed on the resume document.

There are seven key components comprising the Professional Experience section of the resume. These are:

1. Company Name.
2. Company Description.
3. Dates Employed by Company.
4. Job Title.
5. Job Dates.
6. Job Description (including reporting relationship and functional accountability).
7. Key Accomplishments.

From the interview perspective, this is perhaps the most important section of the resume document. How well this section of the resume is written can have significant impact on interview results. If carefully crafted and presented, it will greatly enhance the probability of a successful interview outcome. Conversely, if poorly developed, it can seriously cripple or even destroy employment chances. You will want to pay careful attention to the preparation instructions contained in this section.

Section Format and Content

Before proceeding with a detailed discussion of the content of this section of the resume, it is important that you pay particular attention to the format used in displaying this important component of the resume document. To do this, I strongly recommend that you first spend a few minutes carefully studying the format used in the Professional Experience section on the sample resume presented on page 260.

Note the positioning and treatment of *company employment dates* in relationship to *job dates*. Company employment dates are positioned at the right margin of the resume page and are highlighted in bold type. Job dates, on the other hand, are positioned in parenthesis immediately to the right of the job title and are in normal rather than bold type. Following this simple rule eliminates any possible confusion on the part of the resume reader. Failure to make this visual distinction, however, could lead employers to confuse job and employment dates, causing the reader to falsely conclude that you have been a "job hopper," suggesting that you might be a relatively high employment risk.

Note the difference in the treatment between company names and job titles. Although both employ bold type, company names are set in all capital letters while position titles employ both capital and lowercase letters, with the first letter of each word contained in the job title set in capital letters. This treatment highlights the company name and provides an appropriate visual separation between these two resume elements, facilitating ease of reading and understanding by the employer.

When you have held more than one position with the same employer, company description is normally inserted immediately below company name. When a single job has been held with the same company, however, a brief description of the company can be inserted a single time in the first line of the resume following the job title. In such cases, company description can easily be incorporated as part of the initial statement reflecting your reporting relationship. The following examples should help clarify this point.

Example 1—Multiple Jobs with Same Employer

BRISTOL PAPER COMPANY, Mobile, AL   **1996–2004**
A $3.5 billion market leader in the manufacture and sale of sanitary tissue products including consumer towels, napkins, and facial tissue.

Example 2—Single Job with Same Employer

BRISTOL PAPER COMPANY, Mobile, AL   **1996–2004**
Director of Marketing (2001–2004)
Report to Vice President of Sales and Marketing of this $3.5 billion manufacturer and market leader in the field of sanitary tissue products. Direct staff of 25 with leadership responsibility for new product development, brand management, market research, advertising and promotion ($35 million annual budget). Products include consumer towels, napkins, and facial tissue.

In studying these two sample company descriptions, note the difference in font size. Both company name and position title use 12-point type, while company and job descriptions employ 11-point type. This creates a pleasing visual contrast between resume elements, enhancing both general appearance and ease of readership. Additionally, you may also want to justify text margins to avoid a sloppy, ragged appearance and ensure that right margin text is neatly aligned. This will also enhance the overall appearance of the resume document.

As illustrated in these examples, company description normally includes such items as organization size, products manufactured (or professional services provided), and annual sales volume. Prospective employers want to know what size and type company you worked for so they can assess your probable fit with

their own organization. An employer who is a flooring manufacturer, for example, will want to know whether or not you have had
experience in the flooring industry. If you fail to provide this information, the employer is likely to pass over your resume in favor
of others with flooring industry experience.

You should not automatically assume employers are familiar
with your company. Even when working for large companies such
as DuPont or General Electric, you will still want to show the
products manufactured by the division in which you were employed. Failure to provide this information as part of the company
description may place you at a competitive disadvantage compared to those who have done so. There is clearly a consistent
trend among employers to prefer those with same industry experience, since this cuts down on training time and ensures that the
new hire will "hit the ground running."

The next component of the Professional Experience section
of the resume is the job description. There are five key elements
that should be incorporated into the job description component.
These are:

1. Job Title.
2. Job Dates (i.e., dates employed in that position).
3. Reporting Relationship (i.e., title of person to whom you
   reported).
4. Size and Scope of Position Held (i.e., described in quantitative terms).
5. Functional Responsibility (i.e., specific functions performed or managed).

Although we have previously discussed the treatment and
positioning of job titles on the resume, it is important to comment

further on this subject. In recent years, many employers have elected to use unusual job titles when naming positions. Often this is done in an attempt to better integrate the title chosen with some strategic initiative or organizational culture shift. For example, an employer focusing on creating a team-based culture might call an Engineering Project Manager a Technology Team Facilitator or some other title not commonly used.

Since your resume must communicate with external sources, use of the title Technology Team Facilitator may confuse those unfamiliar with this terminology. Since you want to effectively convey a clear understanding of the position you held, you may wish to substitute the generic job title of Engineering Project Manager to ensure that prospective employers clearly understand the nature of job you held. This is perfectly acceptable practice when writing a resume. When making this kind of change, however, be sure to choose a generic title commonly used and understood within your profession.

When writing a resume, you have a certain amount of license in conveying clear understanding. This is not the case with an employment application, however, where you will need to use exact job titles rather than the generic ones. If ever questioned by an employer about the discrepancy between the job title used on the resume and that used on the formal application, the response is quite simple. Simply explain that you felt use of the generic title better communicated to the outside world the nature of the work you were performing.

When describing your position on the resume, bear in mind that employers will want to know how closely the position you have held parallels the position they are attempting to fill. Key information such as reporting relationship, job size and scope, and functional responsibilities are essential to facilitating this comparison. Take a moment or two to again study the sample job descriptions, as well as those contained in the sample resume contained on page 260, observing how this information is presented.

Begin the job description section by describing your reporting relationship. Starting this section with the words "report to" or "reported to" and then following with your manager's title will simplify the task.

Next, provide a concise description of your functional accountabilities, the key things you were responsible for doing. If you are in a management position, you should list the functional areas you manage. For example, "Functional responsibility includes market research, product development, brand management, advertising, and promotion." If a professional, sole contributor rather than manager, on the other hand, simply cite the key functions you are accountable for performing. For example, "Functional responsibility includes engineering design, installation, start-up, and debugging of consumer tissue and towel papermaking equipment." Administrative support personnel, for example, might state, "Functionally responsible for providing key administrative support including typing and proofing monthly financial statements, preparing PowerPoint presentations, screening incoming mail and e-mail correspondence, arranging executive travel schedules, and meeting setup and coordination."

Future employers will need to have a clear understanding of your functional job responsibilities to determine if you have performed the same or similar work to the position they are filling. The ability to easily make this comparison offers the prospective employer some assurance that you possess the requisite skills and experience essential to successful performance of the position offered.

When formulating your position description, it is also important to include a quantitative description reflecting the size and scope of positions held. Doing so will effectively communicate the scope and complexity of your previous positions. In most cases, the employer is seeking evidence that you have successfully handled positions of comparable size and complexity, enhancing the employer's level of comfort that you are capable of successfully performing the existing job.

If a manager, for example, quantitative descriptions might include the size of your staff, size of budget managed, number of divisions managed, sales volume for which you are accountable, and so on. If you are an Administrative Assistant, for example, the quantitative description might include size of staff served, volume of correspondence processed, volume of records handled, and the like. Such quantitative descriptors will more accurately communicate the size, complexity, and demands of your job, providing the perspective employer with valuable information needed to better assess your fit for the current job opening.

In viewing the sample resume contained on page 260, you can readily see how easy it is to effectively incorporate quantitative data into job descriptions. Note, in particular, how concisely and succinctly this information is presented. There are no wasted words, and yet the employer can quickly grasp the nature and extent of your work experience including reporting relationship, functional responsibilities, and size and scope of positions you have held. The concise way in which this information is presented facilitates ease of readership and yet provides the employer with a clear understanding of the critical elements essential to assessing your qualifications for employment.

The final element in completing the Professional Experience section of the resume document is the Key Accomplishments section. This immediately follows the Job Description and is highlighted through the use of bullet points. From the interview perspective, this is clearly the most important section of the resume when it comes to "making the sale."

In years past, it was sufficient to provide employers with a simple description of your job duties, however, this is no longer the case. In today's competitive environment, managers are heavily focused on employee contribution and productivity. They don't simply want to know "what you are responsible for," they want to know what you have actually done! A simple job description, with no accompanying list of specific accomplishments, is likely to screen you out before you've even begun. Lack of specific resume statements reflecting results you have achieved will place you at a distinct competitive disadvantage.

On the other hand, a resume reflecting a record of continuous accomplishment and significant results will go a long way to "making the sale." It will not only get you in the door, but will also have a major impact on interview results once you are there. Highlighting each of these accomplishments with bullet points will grab the interviewer's attention and focus much of the interview discussion around the key skills and competencies essential to job performance. This is exactly where you want to be. You don't want to waste valuable interview time by requiring the interviewer to dig for this important information.

Because of the critical nature of this resume component, you will want to put considerable thought and effort into developing it. The following directions should help you get off to a good start.

To start the process rolling, list each of the positions you have held on a sheet of paper. Below each job title, list a minimum of four to six major accomplishments or improvements you have achieved while in the position. Copies of old performance evaluations or salary increase summaries should come in handy if you need to jog your memory.

This is often one of the more difficult exercises in resume writing. Often job seekers have difficulty remembering specific achievements and get stuck in the process. If this should happen to you, let me suggest a technique that many, who I have helped write resumes, have successfully used in getting unblocked.

Think about the general state of the position when you first entered it as a new incumbent. What key problems or challenges existed? What improvements were needed? What did you do to address these needs? What specific actions did you take, and what were the results of your efforts?

Once identified and written down on paper, rearrange these accomplishments in relationship to their importance for the type of position you are seeking. List the most important accomplishment first, the second most relevant accomplishment second, the third most important third, and so on, until all have been sorted in accordance with their level of importance to the position you seek. This is the same order in which you will want to list these items on your resume document.

A review of the sample resume on page 260 will illustrate just how easy it is to write key accomplishment statements. There is a formula for writing these accomplishment statements that results in a high level of effectiveness. First, start the accomplishment statement with a verb. This will force you to be concise. A list of common verbs has been provided on the next page. Carefully select the verb that best describes the action you took, such as led, supervised, developed, invented, improved. Try to be as precise as possible in selecting just the right word that best conveys the exact role you played in bringing about a certain end result.

ACTION VERBS

Management Skills

administered
aligned
analyzed
attained
chaired
contracted
consolidated
coordinated
delegated
developed
directed
evaluated
executed
improved
increased
organized
oversaw
planned
prioritized
produced
recommended
reviewed
systematized
scheduled
strengthened
supervised

Communication Skills

addressed
arbitrated
arranged
authored
corresponded
developed
directed
drafted
edited
enlisted
formulated
influenced
interpreted
lectured
mediated
moderated
motivated
negotiated
persuaded
promoted
publicized
recruited
spoke
translated
wrote

Research Skills

analyzed
clarified
collected
critiqued
diagnosed
evaluated
examined
extracted
identified
inspected
interpreted
interviewed
investigated
organized
reviewed
summarized
surveyed

Technical Skills

assembled
built
calculated
computed
designed
devised
engineered
fabricated

maintained
operated
overhauled
programmed
remodeled
repaired
solved
trained
upgraded

Teaching Skills

adapted
advised
clarified
coached
communicated
coordinated
developed
enabled
encouraged
evaluated
explained
facilitated
guided
informed
initiated
instructed
persuaded
set goals
stimulated

Financial Skills

administered
allocated
analyzed
appraised
audited
balanced
budgeted
calculated
computed
developed
forecasted
managed
marketed
planned
projected
researched

Creative Skills

acted
conceptualized
created
designed
developed
directed
established
fashioned
founded
illustrated
instituted
integrated

introduced
invented
originated
performed
planned
revitalized
shaped

Helping Skills

assessed
assisted
clarified
coached
counseled
demonstrated
diagnosed
educated
expedited
facilitated
familiarized
guided
referred
represented
trained

**Clerical or
Detail Skills**

approved
arranged
catalogued
classified
collected

compiled	operated	retrieved
dispatched	organized	screened
executed	prepared	specified
generated	processed	systematized
implemented	proofread	tabulated
inspected	purchased	typed
monitored	recorded	validated

Second, use quantitative results statements that clearly convey to the employer the degree of improvement you brought in each instance. For example, simply stating that you increased sales has little impact on the reader. Telling the employer that you increased sales by 200 percent over the first two years, however, is bound to get the reader's attention. There is a huge difference. With this example, you can readily see how much more powerful an accomplishment statement becomes when it is supported by quantitative dimensions that convey the level or degree of improvement you brought.

If you experience difficulty remembering an exact number or percentage, qualify the statistic by using the words *approximately* or *about*, so long as you know the numeric you are using is "in the ballpark." For example, you could state, "Reduced operating costs by approximately 30 percent in the first year." This is far better than simply stating, "Reduced operating costs in the first year."

When reviewing the sample resume at the end of this chapter, you will note that each accomplishment statement is preceded by a bullet. This highlights the statement, drawing the reader's attention.

If you have been thoughtful in crafting your accomplishment statements, you are likely to realize the full benefit of your efforts during the course of your employment interviews. Since employers frequently use the resume as an interview roadmap, systematically probing each position held and results achieved, your extra effort is bound to pay large dividends. As employers probe these key accomplishments in greater detail, you are afforded an excellent opportunity to showcase your strongest skills and competencies.

If written particularly well, these achievement statements will do most of the selling for you. The resume will automatically document a solid history of achievement and results, providing a convincing and compelling story that should encourage the employer to hire you.

Since you will want to commit most of the resume to describing your most recent positions, it is unnecessary to provide much detail on positions held earlier in your career. In fact, earlier positions are of little interest to employers so they deserve no more than a simple listing of job titles and dates. There is no need to include a description of the position and list of accomplishments. Doing so serves no real purpose other than to lengthen the resume and present a greater barrier to readership.

If, in fact, you are an older worker, listing early positions along with employment dates is a dead giveaway to your age, inviting age discrimination. If this is your situation, you may want to give consideration to eliminating these earlier positions from the resume entirely. In this way you can disguise your age, all but eliminating the possibility of age discrimination and increasing the probability of landing job interviews. If later questioned by an employer as to why you didn't list these positions on the resume, your answer is both honest and simple. Tell the employer, "Since there is limited space on the resume, I felt it important to use this space to more fully describe my most recent positions, rather than to list positions that have little or no relevance to my current job search objective. Additionally, quite frankly, I wished to eliminate the possibility of age discrimination. I'm sure you can appreciate this." Such explanation is likely to cause the issue to evaporate rather quickly.

Section 4—Education

As illustrated on the sample resume on page 260, the Education section of the resume lists the degree and major, followed by school and date of graduation. List highest level degree first. Additionally for esthetic purposes, I recommend you center the educational data under the Education heading as shown in the following example:

EDUCATION

Ph.D., Physical Organic Chemistry, University of Colorado, 2002
M.S., Organic Chemistry, University of Utah, 1999
B.S., Chemistry, Bucknell University, 1997

Section 5—Professional Memberships

As stated previously, Professional Memberships is an optional resume component. Avoid listing extraneous memberships that have no relevance to the position for which you are applying. Stick to job relevant professional memberships only. As with the Education section, you will want to center the professional memberships under the Professional Memberships component as shown below:

PROFESSIONAL MEMBERSHIPS

National Pest Management Association, President, 2001–2002
National Pest Management Association, Member, 1996–2002
Professional Lawn Care Association, Member, 1990–2002
Gold Course Superintendents Association, Member, 1990–2002

This section of the resume might also be used to list professional certifications earned, professional awards received, special recognition received, offices held in relevant professional or trade associations, and other appropriate items lending testimony to your qualifications as a professional in your field. You may want to change the resume section heading to a title that more appropriately fits the category. Optional titles might include Professional Affiliations, Professional Recognition, Honors and Awards, or other appropriate titles.

Section 6—Patents

If you are a technical professional and hold relevant patents, you will want to show these on your resume. This provides strong testimony to your technical genius and creativity. This is particularly true if multiple patents have been issued in your name.

On the other hand, if the only patents you hold were issued many years ago and you have not been awarded a patent in recent years, you may want to think twice about even listing patents on the resume at all. To do so might well suggest to a prospective employer you are no longer the technical genius you once were, or that you have contributed little to your employer in recent years. You want to avoid the possibility of being labeled a "has been," and should consider dropping the Patents section from your resume entirely or simply not show dates of patent issue.

As with the Education and Professional Memberships sections of the resume, you will want to center patent listings under the *Patents* heading, rather than flush with the left margin. Patent listings should include both the patent number and title as shown in the following example:

PATENTS

US Patent 7,249,247 - Gravity Feed Conveyor System with High-Speed Process Capability

US Patent 7,189,232 - Bar Code Palletizing System with Computerized Sorting Control

US Patent 6,994,249 - Transpiration Sheet Drying Using Through-Air Conveyor System

SECTION 7—AWARDS AND RECOGNITION

As with previous resume sections, if you decide to list special awards and recognition received, list only those that are truly relevant to the position for which you are applying. Also, as with the Patents section, do not show only those awards received years ago, especially if you have had no special awards or recognition in recent years. Absence of recognition in recent years may give the wrong message to a prospective employer, suggesting you are no longer the high performer you were earlier in your career. This is not a message you want to send!

Also, if you are midcareer, don't show that you were named captain of your high school football team 30 years ago. This is utter foolishness and will suggest to employers that you lack appropriate judgment and common sense. Likewise, if you were named president of the local school board, don't show this on your resume if you are applying for a job as a research scientist. There is no relevance to the position for which you are applying. Cite only job-relevant honors and awards.

Your listing of special recognition and rewards should be centered under the Awards and Recognition section of the resume. The typical way of presenting this data is to simply list the name of the award or recognition, and the awarding organization, followed by date received. The following is an example of a typical Awards and Recognition resume presentation:

AWARDS AND RECOGNITION

President's Award for Outstanding Contribution, Procter & Gamble, 1998, 1999, 2004
Employee of the Year Award, Procter & Gamble, 1999
Top Sales Producer, East Coast Division, Kimberly Clark Corporation, 1996, 1997, 1998

WRITING TRICKS AND TECHNIQUES

Careful review of the sample resume at the end of this chapter shows that certain writing tricks and techniques were employed to make this resume a brief, concise, and relatively forceful document. Note how the resume's author employed these techniques and apply these same simple approaches when writing your own resume document. You should find these techniques particularly beneficial in improving the overall quality and impact of your resume document.

- Use of articles (e.g., a, an, and the) is unnecessary and should, for the most part, be eliminated. They add no real meaning or clarity to the resume.

- Eliminate use of personal pronouns (i.e., he, she, me, you, they, them, us). Such pronouns are unnecessary in a resume and tend to distract from its impact and forcefulness.

- There is no need to use complete sentences when writing a resume. Highly descriptive phrases and clauses can communicate quite effectively, and consume far less space.

- Be concise. Eliminate all unnecessary words from the resume. If a word adds little meaning or clarity to a statement, simply delete it. It adds no real value to the document.

- Begin most resume sentences and statements with a verb. Doing so will force brevity and conciseness.

Hopefully this chapter has provided you with a good understanding of what is important in preparing an effective resume document. You will find the advice presented to be professionally sound and, if followed, your resume document will significantly enhance your overall interview effectiveness. I have provided the same resume advice to thousands of job seekers who have gone through our corporate career transition programs, and can tell you that many hundreds have specifically commented that their resumes played a key role in landing job offers.

CATHERINE S. DAVIDSON

1604 Riverside Drive
Irvine, CA 18274   *Cadav@AOL.com*

(816) 557-0925 Home
(816) 957-4075 Cell

PROFILE

Senior marketing executive with consistent success in developing and establishing new and existing chemical brands as market leaders in their product category. Strong market research, brand management, advertising and promotional expertise. A strategic thinker noted for outstanding leadership, team-building, customer relations, and presentation skills.

PROFESSIONAL EXPERIENCE

BAXTER CHEMICAL COMPANY, Oceanside, CA   **1996-Present**

Leading, $6.5 billion, 28,000 employee manufacturer and distributor of chemical specialties with 8 manufacturing plants in the U.S. and distribution facilities in over 35 countries worldwide.

Vice President of Marketing (2002-Present)

Report to the President and CEO with functional responsibility for product development, market research, brand management, advertising and promotion for over 130 specialty chemicals sold principally to the steel, automotive, and electronics markets. Direct staff of 30 professionals with annual budget of $130 million.

- Led development of 12 new specialty products sold to the cable industry, generating $380 million in new revenue in just under 2 years.
- Revamped steel industry marketing strategy, propelling Baxter from #4 industry supplier to #2, resulting in over $240 million in new sales within 1 year.
- Spearheaded sale of paint chemicals division to Wilson Paint Specialties for $180 million, reducing corporate overhead by over 15% and dropping nearly $20 million annually to the bottom line.
- Led breakthrough effort in the automotive specialties market, capturing 3 major accounts (GM, Ford and Chrysler), accounting for $10 million annual revenue increase.
- Reorganized marketing division reducing headcount by 10% ($2 million savings).

Director of Marketing – Steel Specialties (1999-2002)

Reported to Vice President of Marketing with full marketing responsibility for chemical specialties sold to the steel industry ($2.1 billion annual sales). Functional responsibility for product development, market research, brand management, advertising, and promotion (12 professionals, $62 million budget).

- Led development and market introduction of 6 new chemical specialties for steel coating, generating $420 million in new revenue and capturing nearly 25% market share in 3 years.
- Convinced management to re-price the entire steel coating product line, offering tiered volume discounts that resulted in a 20% increase in sales volume and 5% increase in sales revenue.

Catherine S. Davidson   Page 2

- Implemented sophisticated competitor tracking and intelligence gathering process, allowing company to predict and counter major shifts in competitor marketing strategy before they occur.
- Reorganized department, building strong, cohesive, effective team that significantly upgraded the image of the marketing department and increased its credibility with the senior management team.

Senior Brand Manager – Steel Specialties (1996-1999)
Hired by Director of Marketing – Steel Specialties to focus on the declining steel coatings market with the goal of improving market position and increasing sales. Managed 2 Brand Managers and a $6 million budget.

- Implemented new strategic initiatives that raised company's market leadership position from # 6 to # 4 and increased market penetration by 18%.
- Increased sales by 15% in less than 1 year.
- Introduced new market analysis software and improved methodology that greatly enhanced accuracy of market analysis and projections, bringing increased credibility to the function.

WILSON CHEMICAL SPECIALTIES, INC., Cherry Hill, N.J.   **1992-1996**
A $950 million, 4,500 employee manufacturer and distributor of specialty chemicals to the electronics industry.

Brand Manager (1994-1996)
Reported to Director of Marketing with responsibility for developing and implementing new brand strategies for the company's specialty chemicals sold to the computer and telecommunication industries.

Associate Brand Manager (1992-1994)

EDUCATION

M.B.A., Marketing, Michigan State University, 1992
B.S., Mechanical Engineering, University of Michigan, 1990

AWARDS & RECOGNITION

Chairman's Award for Outstanding Performance, Baxter Chemical, 2001 & 2003
Employee of the Year Award, Wilson Chemical, 1996
Wilson Chemical Academic Scholarship Award, 1987, 1988, & 1990

Index